Test Your Bridge Play

Edwin B. Kantar

*115 Declarer-Play Problems Designed to Improve
Card Playing Techniques for Bridge Players
Who Are Sick and Tired of Going
Down in Cold Contracts.*

Published by
Melvin Powers
WILSHIRE BOOK COMPANY
12015 Sherman Road
No. Hollywood, California 91605
Telephone: (213) 875-1711 / (818) 983-1105

Printed by

HAL LEIGHTON PRINTING COMPANY
P.O. Box 3952
North Hollywood, California 91605
Telephone: (213) 983-1105

Library of Congress Catalog Card Number: 74-84310
ISBN 0-87980-390-8
Printed in the United States of America

CONTENTS

INTRODUCTION

This book was not designed for expert players. However, nobody will ever become an expert until they can handle the types of hands that are presented here.

The hands are designed for players who would like to improve their play of the cards relatively painlessly.

Most of the problems have mates. In other words you will have more than one opportunity to grapple with an end play or an avoidance play. In fact the book was written with just that in mind—seeing if the reader can learn to RECOGNIZE hand types as he sifts through the book.

At the end of this book each problem will be categorized by its central theme or themes.

What the reader should do is carefully mark which problems have given him trouble. He should then check to see if they have a central theme. In that way he will determine which areas need to be stressed.

These problems contain NO catches. They are all straightforward. The reader is asked to forget temporarily the word "overtricks". Just worry about making the contract. Do not get greedy. Play each hand as safely as possible.

It has always been my feeling that most players who rush into tournament bridge because it is more fun and/or social than rubber bridge have missed out on the fundamental nature of the play of the cards.

Rubber bridge or money players do not worry about overtricks—neither do Team of Four players. They only think in terms of making their contract. It is a good habit to form. Later you can start worrying about overtricks.

The bidding is fairly straightforward. Anytime a convention, even a simple one like Stayman, is used, it is noted.

As at the table, one should pay particular attention to what the opponents have or have not bid. Original passes are important as are opening leads and the subsequent revelation of honor card holdings in the opponents' hands. It is assumed that the defenders are leading fourth best and king from ace-king.

You can feel you are making progress if you err on a particular theme the first time that type of hand appears, but pick it up when it reappears. It will reappear—not to haunt you—to help you.

Finally, if you have a friend and/or a partner who is tired of going down in cold contracts, give him/her this book. You couldn't do them a bigger favor—he said modestly.

Edwin Kantar

(1) FIRST THINGS FIRST

East-West vulnerable
Dealer South

North

♠ A
♡ 10 9 8 7
♢ A Q 3 2
♣ K Q J 5

South

♠ Q J 10 9 8 7 6
♡ A 6 5
♢ 4
♣ 8 6

South	West	North	East
3 ♠	Pass	4 ♠	All Pass

Opening lead: ♡ K

East plays the deuce. What is your plan?

FIRST THINGS FIRST (SOLUTION)

North

♠ A
♡ 10 9 8 7
◇ A Q 3 2
♣ K Q J 5

West	East
♠ K 4	♠ 5 3 2
♡ K Q J	♡ 4 3 2
◇ K 9 8 6 5	◇ J 10 7
♣ 10 4 3	♣ A 9 7 2

South

♠ Q J 10 9 8 7 6
♡ A 6 5
◇ 4
♣ 8 6

Counting losers, (the FIRST thing you do at a suit contract) you see that you could lose one spade (unless the king is singleton—don't hold your breath) two hearts and a club for a grand total of FOUR.

You don't have TIME to work with the clubs because upon winning the club ace the opponents will simply cash their two heart tricks. Keep in mind that East played the DEUCE of hearts at trick one, denying a doubleton. Therefore, holding up the first round of hearts, intending to win the second and knock out the ace of clubs simply won't work. As long as hearts are 3-3 it doesn't matter who has the ace of clubs, the opponents will be able to collect two hearts and a club along with their spade trick. No, clubs is not the answer.

The answer is to take the diamond finesse at trick two! No need to duck a round of hearts, East may have a singleton. What fun if you duck the opening lead and East ruffs the second heart. What fun for them.

If the diamond finesse works, you can discard a losing heart on the ace of diamonds and eventually lose a spade, a heart and a club. If the diamond finesse loses, you go down two. Big deal. Isn't it worth an extra 50 points to try to make a game contract?

KEY LESSON POINTERS

1. COUNT YOUR LOSERS IN A SUIT CONTRACT. IF YOU HAVE MORE THAN YOU CAN AFFORD, LOOK AROUND FOR A PLACE TO DUMP SOME OF THEM—SETTING UP LONG SUITS, FINESSES ETC.
2. WATCH THIRD HAND'S SIGNAL AT TRICK ONE. IT GIVES YOU AN IDEA OF HOW THE SUIT LED IS DIVIDING AS WELL AS THE LOCATION OF THE MISSING HONORS.

(2) RECOGNITION

East-West vulnerable
Dealer North

North
♠ 6 4 2
♡ A 10 2
♢ K J 10 9
♣ K 9 2

South
♠ A Q 5
♡ J
♢ A Q 8 6 4 3
♣ A Q 8

North	East	South	West
Pass	Pass	1 ♢	Pass
3 ♢	Pass	6 ♢	All Pass

Opening lead: ♡ K

Not being one to monkey around in the bidding, you bid the slam directly. Now all you have to do is make it. Plan the play.

RECOGNITION (Solution)

North
♠ 6 4 2
♡ A 10 2
♦ K J 10 9
♣ K 9 2

West
♠ K 10 7 3
♡ K Q 9 8
♦ 5 2
♣ 10 5 3

East
♠ J 9 8
♡ 7 6 5 4 3
♦ 7
♣ J 7 6 4

South
♠ A Q 5
♡ J
♦ A Q 8 6 4 3
♣ A Q 8

You should see at a glance that your only losers (two possible) are in spades. Your objective should be to AVOID the spade finesse, or at least postpone it as long as possible.

Whenever you have an A Q combination you should direct your efforts at forcing your left hand opponent to lead the suit into your ace-queen. This frequently means giving him the lead in another suit to force the lead in the suit you want led.

Consider the opening lead. West should have both honors in hearts. The hand lends itself to a strip and end play. It has the ingredients. Good trumps on both sides, a club suit that can easily be eliminated from both hands, a suit you do not want to lead yourself, (spades) and a suit that you can throw your left hand opponent in with, (hearts).

Win the ace of hearts, draw trumps, ruff the deuce of hearts, play three rounds of clubs ending in dummy and lead the ten of hearts discarding a spade, a loser in any case.

West, on lead with the queen of hearts, will either have to lead a spade into your ace-queen or give you a ruff and a sluff by leading a fourth heart.

KEY LESSON POINTERS

1. ALWAYS LOOK FOR WAYS TO AVOID FINESSES IN SHORT SUITS THAT ARE EQUALLY DIVIDED BETWEEN YOUR HAND AND DUMMY.
2. HANDS THAT HAVE STRONG TRUMP HOLDINGS ON BOTH SIDES WITH NO LONG SUIT TO ESTABLISH LEND THEMSELVES TO THROW-IN AND END PLAYS.

(3) TWO KINGS MISSING

Both sides vulnerable
Dealer South

North
- ♠ A Q J 7
- ♡ K 10 8 5
- ◇ A Q 5 4
- ♣ A

South
- ♠ 4 2
- ♡ A Q J 9 7 6 3 2
- ◇ 7
- ♣ 10 8

South	West	North	East
4 ♡	Pass	4 NT	Pass
5 ◇	Pass	7 ♡	All Pass

Opening lead: ♣ K

Your partner was hoping you had three clubs in which case there should be thirteen tricks; eight hearts, three aces plus two club ruffs in dummy. The best laid plans...

Plan your play in this vulnerable grand slam.

TWO KINGS MISSING (Solution)

North

♠ A Q J 7
♡ K 10 8 5
◇ A Q 5 4
♣ A

West

♠ 10 8 6 5
♡ —
◇ J 9 8 6 3
♣ K Q J 4

East

♠ K 9 3
♡ 4
◇ K 10 2
♣ 9 7 6 5 3 2

South

♠ 4 2
♡ A Q J 9 7 6 3 2
◇ 7
♣ 10 8

Your only possible loser is in spades—but you have three possible ways of getting rid of it! (1) You can take the spade finesse (2) You can take the diamond finesse (3) You can try to ruff out the king of diamonds and if it does not drop doubleton or third, you can take the spade finesse.

Obviously (3) is best and that is what you should do.

KEY LESSON POINTERS

1. WHEN FACED WITH A CHOICE OF TWO SIDE-SUIT FINESSES FOR A KING, EITHER OF WHICH WILL GIVE YOU YOUR CONTRACT, FIRST ATTACK THE SUIT THAT HAS THE SINGLETON AND TRY TO RUFF OUT THE KING IN THAT SUIT. IF THAT DOES NOT SUCCEED, TAKE THE FINESSE IN THE OTHER SUIT.

   WITH NO SINGLETON IN EITHER SUIT, PLAY THE ACE OF THE LONGER SUIT, AND IF THE KING HAS NOT DROPPED, FINESSE IN THE SHORTER SUIT.

(4) CAREFUL!

Both sides vulnerable
Dealer East

North

♠ 4 3
♡ 5 3 2
◇ Q 10 9 8 3
♣ A J 2

South

♠ A 10 7
♡ A 8 6
◇ A J 6 5
♣ K Q 10

East	South	West	North
3 ♠	3 NT	All Pass	

Opening lead: ♠ 5

East plays the J ♠ . Plan the play.

CAREFUL! (Solution)

North

♠ 4 3
♡ 5 3 2
♢ Q 10 9 8 3
♣ A J 2

West

♠ 5
♡ K 10 7 4
♢ K 7 2
♣ 8 7 6 5 4

East

♠ K Q J 9 8 6 2
♡ Q J 9
♢ 4
♣ 9 3

South

♠ A 10 7
♡ A 8 6
♢ A J 6 5
♣ K Q 10

East is marked with a seven card spade suit on the bidding and there is a great danger if you duck the opening lead, East may find a heart switch. If he does, and if the king of diamonds resides with West you have just mangled a cold hand.

The answer is NOT to give East a chance to find the killing heart switch. Win the opening lead, cross to dummy with the jack of clubs and run the queen of diamonds.

Assuming this loses and West has no more spades you have nine tricks. What if West produces a second spade? Simple. You are down two!

However, (1) East is unlikely to have six spades for a vulnerable THREE bid, and even if West does have a second spade and you duck the opening lead, East can always switch to a heart at trick two rather than continue a spade with no outside entry.

KEY LESSON POINTERS

1. TRY TO WORK OUT THE DISTRIBUTION OF THE SUIT LED FROM THE BIDDING AND THE OPENING LEAD.
2. THERE IS NO REASON TO MAKE A HOLD-UP PLAY WHEN YOU KNOW THAT ONE OF THE OPPONENTS HAS NO MORE CARDS IN THE SUIT BEING LED.
3. YOU MUST BE ALIVE TO THE POSSIBILITY OF A DAMAGING SHIFT IN YET ANOTHER WEAK SUIT WHEN YOU MAKE A HOLD-UP PLAY.
4. WHEN AN OPPONENT OPENS FIRST SEAT WITH A VULNERABLE THREE BID ASSUME A SEVEN CARD SUIT.

(5) MARKED

Neither side vulnerable
Dealer West

North
♠ 10 7 4 3 2
♡ Q 5 4
♢ A Q 8
♣ 3 2

South
♠ A K Q 9 8
♡ 8 7 6
♢ 10 2
♣ K J 7

West	North	East	South
Pass	Pass	Pass	1 ♠
2 ♡	2 ♠	All Pass	

Opening lead: ♡ K

East plays high-low in hearts and ruffs West's deuce of hearts at trick three. At trick four East shifts to the five of clubs. Which club do you play from your hand?

MARKED (Solution)

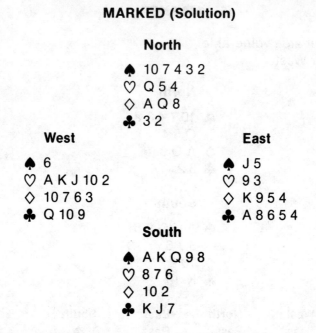

North
♠ 10 7 4 3 2
♡ Q 5 4
◇ A Q 8
♣ 3 2

West
♠ 6
♡ A K J 10 2
◇ 10 7 6 3
♣ Q 10 9

East
♠ J 5
♡ 9 3
◇ K 9 5 4
♣ A 8 6 5 4

South
♠ A K Q 9 8
♡ 8 7 6
◇ 10 2
♣ K J 7

West has passed originally and has turned up with A K J 10x of hearts. He cannot have the ace of clubs or else he would have opened the bidding. You should go up with the king of clubs. East is marked with the club ace.

KEY LESSON POINTERS

1. WHEN A PLAYER PASSES ORIGINALLY AND TURNS UP WITH A STRONG FIVE OR SIX CARD SUIT HEADED BY THE HIGH HONORS, IT IS A VIRTUAL CERTAINTY THAT HE HAS NO OTHER ACE OR KING.

(6) PATIENCE

Neither side vulnerable
Dealer East

North
♠ A J 10
♡ 7 3
♢ A 10 9 6 5
♣ K 4 3

South
♠ K 8 7 6
♡ 5 2
♢ K Q J 8 7
♣ A 2

East	South	West	North
Pass	1 ♢	4 ♡	5 ♢
All Pass			

Opening lead: ♡ K

West cashes two hearts, East playing the ten and nine. At trick three West shifts to a trump and you play a second trump East discarding a spade.

Now you play ace-king and ruff a club, all following. How do you play the spades?

PATIENCE (Solution)

North
♠ A J 10
♡ 7 3
◇ A 10 9 6 5
♣ K 4 3

West
♠ 5
♡ A K Q J 8 6 4
◇ 3 2
♣ Q 10 9

East
♠ Q 9 4 3 2
♡ 10 9
◇ 4
♣ J 8 7 6 5

South
♠ K 8 7 6
♡ 5 2
◇ K Q J 8 7
♣ A 2

Have you been counting? Whenever you come across a hand that depends upon a two-way finesse for a queen it will usually be a counting hand.

If you can possibly delay the play of the two-way suit (spades) until you get information about the other suits, it stands to reason you will be better off.

For example, West's bid of four hearts along with East's high-low in hearts indicates that West started with a SEVEN card heart suit.

West did follow to two diamonds and three clubs so he can have no more than one spade. Cash the ace of spades and run the jack through East. He must have the queen.

KEY LESSON POINTERS

1. USE THEIR BIDDING AND SIGNALLING TO HELP YOU COUNT A HAND.
2. HANDS WHERE ONE OR BOTH PLAYERS HAVE MADE A PREEMPTIVE BID ARE EASIER TO COUNT. ONCE YOU HAVE DISCOVERED THAT ONE PLAYER HAS A LONG SUIT, COUNT THAT HAND. YOU DO NOT HAVE TO COUNT BOTH HANDS!
3. IF YOU SEE THAT THE CONTRACT REVOLVES AROUND ONE PARTICULAR SUIT, TRY TO DELAY THE PLAY OF THAT SUIT UNTIL YOU CAN RESEARCH THE OTHER SUITS.
4. TAKE YOUR TIME WHEN YOU ARE COUNTING A HAND. DON'T PANIC, OR AT LEAST DON'T LET THEM KNOW YOU ARE PANICKING.

(7)   MAKING NINE EIGHT

North-South vulnerable
Dealer North

North
♠ 3
♡ A J 8 6 4
♢ A K Q J 2
♣ K J

South
♠ K Q 6 4
♡ 3
♢ 7 6 5
♣ A 8 7 6 4

North	East	South	West
1 ♡	Pass	1 ♠	Pass
3 ♢	Pass	3 NT	All Pass

Opening lead: ♣ 2

Plan the play.

MAKING NINE EIGHT (Solution)

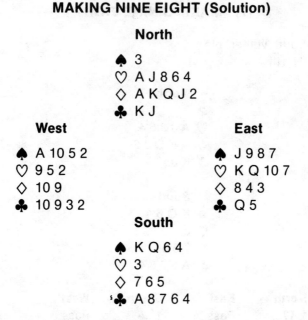

North
- ♠ 3
- ♡ A J 8 6 4
- ♢ A K Q J 2
- ♣ K J

West
- ♠ A 10 5 2
- ♡ 9 5 2
- ♢ 10 9
- ♣ 10 9 3 2

East
- ♠ J 9 8 7
- ♡ K Q 10 7
- ♢ 8 4 3
- ♣ Q 5

South
- ♠ K Q 6 4
- ♡ 3
- ♢ 7 6 5
- ♣ A 8 7 6 4

You have nine tricks—don't compress them into eight! Count. You have five diamonds, two clubs and one heart trick off the top with an easy ninth trick possible in spades—so what's the problem?

The problem is greed and/or no planning. In order to develop your ninth trick in spades you need a sure REENTRY to your own hand. You have exactly that in the form of the ace of clubs.

You should play the KING of clubs at trick one, reserving the ace of clubs as the FUTURE entry to the spades. If you play the jack of clubs and East produces the queen—nine tricks have suddenly become eight!

KEY LESSON POINTERS

1. DON'T MAKE A MOVE AT A NO TRUMP CONTRACT UNTIL YOU COUNT YOUR SURE TRICKS.
2. IF YOU MUST DEVELOP ADDITIONAL TRICKS CONSIDER THE POSSIBLE ENTRY PROBLEMS.
3. CONSERVE ENTRIES TO THE WEAKER HAND IF THE TRICKS YOU ARE ESTABLISHING ARE IN THE WEAKER HAND.
4. FIRST SECURE YOUR CONTRACT, WORRY ABOUT OVER-TRICKS LATER.

(8) A TALE OF TWO KINGS

East-West vulnerable
Dealer South

North
♠ 8 6 3 2
♡ 7 5
◇ A 10 7 6
♣ A Q J

South
♠ K 5
♡ A K 4
◇ K 9 8 4 3
♣ K 7 3

South	West	North	East
1 NT	Pass	3 NT	All Pass

Opening lead: ♡ Q

East plays the three of hearts. Plan the play.

A TALE OF TWO KINGS (Solution)

North

♠ 8 6 3 2
♡ 7 5
♢ A 10 7 6
♣ A Q J

West	East
♠ A 7 4	♠ Q J 10 9
♡ Q J 10 6 2	♡ 9 8 3
♢ J	♢ Q 5 2
♣ 10 8 6 5	♣ 9 4 2

South

♠ K 5
♡ A K 4
♢ K 9 8 4 3
♣ K 7 3

Yes, your partner forgot to bid 2 ♣, Stayman. Yes, you might have had four spades to go along with his four spades. Nobody is perfect.

You have five sure tricks outside of diamonds, your best suit, Therefore you only need four diamond tricks which should not prove to be a problem.

The problem is that you are vulnerable to an attack in SPADES from East. EAST is the danger hand and you must try to keep East off lead. Win the first heart with the KING, lead a club to dummy and run the ten of diamonds (safety play in case either opponent has QJxx) into the West hand. Assume the ten loses, you have four diamond tricks and your king of spades is safe!

KEY LESSON POINTERS

1. LEARN TO LOOK AT YOUR HAND AND DUMMY AS AN ENTIRE UNIT. TRY NOT TO CONCENTRATE ON JUST ONE SUIT, BUT ON EVERY SUIT IN RELATION TO EVERY OTHER SUIT. (OF COURSE, IF YOU COULD DO THAT YOU WOULDN'T HAVE TO READ THIS BOOK.)

2. WHEN A QUEEN IS LED VS. NO TRUMP AND YOU HAVE BOTH THE ACE AND KING IN YOUR HAND AND DECIDE TO WIN THE TRICK, IT IS ALMOST ALWAYS RIGHT TO WIN WITH THE KING. YOUR RIGHT HAND OPPONENT WILL NEVER BE COMPLETELY SURE WHO HAS THE ACE AS HIS PARTNER MIGHT HAVE BEEN LEADING FROM AN AQJ COMBINATION. IF YOU WIN WITH THE ACE YOUR RIGHT HAND OPPONENT WILL KNOW THAT YOU REMAIN WITH THE KING.

3. IF YOU HAVE A KING IN ONE HAND OPPOSITE SMALL CARDS IN THE OTHER, BE THANKFUL THE SUIT WASN'T LED—BUT MAKE SURE THAT IF IT IS, THE LEAD WILL BE COMING UP TO THE KING—NOT THROUGH IT!

(9) TOUGH LEAD

Neither side vulnerable
Dealer South

North
♠ 2
♡ Q J 10
◇ Q 9 8 6
♣ A Q 9 5 3

South
♠ A 9 7 5 4
♡ A K 9 8 7
◇ 3 2
♣ 4

South	West	North	East
1 ♠	Pass	2 ♣	Pass
2 ♡	Pass	2 NT	Pass
3 ♡	Pass	4 ♡	All Pass

Opening lead: ♡ 3

East follows, plan the play.

TOUGH LEAD (Solution)

North

♠ 2
♡ Q J 10
♢ Q 9 8 6
♣ A Q 9 5 3

West

♠ Q 10 8 6
♡ 5 3
♢ A 10
♣ K 10 7 6 2

East

♠ K J 3
♡ 6 4 2
♢ K J 7 5 4
♣ J 8

South

♠ A 9 7 5 4
♡ A K 9 8 7
♢ 3 2
♣ 4

Without a trump lead you would have ten tricks. Five hearts in your own hand, two black aces, and three spade ruffs in dummy.

With the trump lead you have nine tricks so you must take the club finesse. Also, you must take it early as you have no convenient hand reentry after you ruff a spade other than a club ruff.

Overtake the heart, finesse the queen of clubs, cash the ace of clubs, discarding either a diamond or a spade, and cross ruff the black suits for ten tricks.

KEY LESSON POINTERS

1. WHEN BOTH HANDS HAVE SHORT SUITS CONSIDER THE POSSIBILITY OF A CROSSRUFF.
2. WHEN PLAYING A CROSSRUFF, COUNT TRICKS, NOT LOSERS.
3. BEFORE EMBARKING UPON A CROSSRUFF, CASH YOUR SIDE SUIT WINNERS FIRST. SIDE WINNERS MIGHT NOT LIVE LATER AS THE OPPONENTS DO HAVE A CHANCE TO DISCARD WHEN YOU CROSSRUFF.
4. THE TRICK IS TO KNOW EXACTLY HOW MANY SIDE WINNERS YOU NEED TO CASH BEFORE EMBARKING UPON YOR CROSS-RUFF. BY COUNTING THE NUMBER OF TRUMP TRICKS YOU WILL SCORE BY CROSSRUFFING, YOU WILL KNOW THE NUMBER OF SIDE SUIT WINNERS YOU NEED.

(10) LOOK FOR HELP

Both sides vulnerable
Dealer South

North
♠ A Q 8
♡ J 8 7 6 3
♦ K 4 3
♣ A 3

South
♠ 4 3
♡ A K 10 9 4 2
♦ J 6 5
♣ 9 8

South	West	North	East
2 ♡*	Dbl.	4 ♡	All Pass

*Weak Two Bid

Opening lead: ♣ King

East plays the deuce. Plan the play.

LOOK FOR HELP (Solution)

North

♠ A Q 8
♡ J 8 7 6 3
◇ K 4 3
♣ A 3

West

♠ K J 10 9
♡ Q
◇ Q 10 9 2
♣ K Q J 6

East

♠ 7 6 5 2
♡ 5
◇ A 8 7
♣ 10 7 5 4 2

South

♠ 4 3
♡ A K 10 9 4 2
◇ J 6 5
♣ 9 8

There are five possible losers! One spade, three diamonds and a club. Don't go away. West has done some strong bidding and should have some of the missing high cards which will help eliminate some of those five losers.

The important points to note are: (1) you absolutely need the king of spades with West to make the contract. (2) diamonds is a suit you prefer to have led to you rather than vice versa. (3) clubs are evenly divided between your hand and dummy. Suits with losers that are evenly divided lend themselves to throw-in possibilities.

Proper procedure is to win the club, draw trumps, finesse the queen of spades, cash the ace of spades, ruff a spade and exit with a club. Whoever wins will either have to play diamonds for you, thus insuring you of one trick (play low if West leads one) in diamonds and your contract, or give you a ruff and a sluff also at the cost of a trick.

KEY LESSON POINTERS

1. Whenever you have a critical suit—a suit you want the opponents to lead first —(diamonds)—, and an equal length suit (clubs) that has a built-in loser there exists the possibility of using the equal length loser as the throw-in card.

2. However, for a throw-in to succeed, you must first draw trumps leaving trumps in both your hand and dummy, and eliminate all safe exit cards in the fourth suit—(spades). Finally the stage is set for the throw-in.

3. Equal length suits, such as clubs on this hand, are no good for establishing discards but are quite valuable as throw-in suits.

(11) COUNTERMEASURES

Neither side vulnerable
Dealer North

North
♠ A 6 4
♡ Q
◇ K Q J 9 8 4 3
♣ 7 5

South
♠ K Q J 10 9 8
♡ J 3
◇ A
♣ K J 6 2

North	East	South	West
1 ◇	Pass	1 ♠	Dbl.
2 ◇	Pass	4 ♠	All Pass

Opening lead: ♡ K

At trick two West continues with the ace of hearts. What is your plan?

COUNTERMEASURES (Solution)

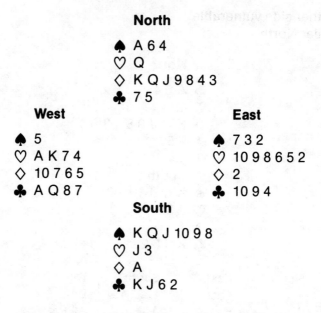

North
- ♠ A 6 4
- ♡ Q
- ◇ K Q J 9 8 4 3
- ♣ 7 5

West
- ♠ 5
- ♡ A K 7 4
- ◇ 10 7 6 5
- ♣ A Q 8 7

East
- ♠ 7 3 2
- ♡ 10 9 8 6 5 2
- ◇ 2
- ♣ 10 9 4

South
- ♠ K Q J 10 9 8
- ♡ J 3
- ◇ A
- ♣ K J 6 2

Your plan should be to use dummy's diamonds to discard clubs rather than ruff clubs in the dummy.

The problem is, of course, that diamonds are blocked, and if you ruff the heart lead in dummy you will be at the mercy of a 2-2 spade division. How else can you use those diamonds unless you draw trumps ending in dummy. What if the spades are not 2-2? Need you ask?

The answer is NOT to ruff the second heart. Simply discard a club. If West wants his ace of clubs, he had better take it. If he plays anything else, you can win in your hand, cash the ace of diamonds and then play THREE rounds of spades ending in dummy. Now you can savor your diamonds in peace.

KEY LESSON POINTERS

1. THERE IS NO RULE THAT SAYS YOU HAVE TO RUFF IN DUMMY IF IT WILL PREVENT YOU FROM RUNNING A LONG SUIT.
2. WHEN PLANNING TO USE A LONG SIDE SUIT IN DUMMY WITH ONLY ONE ENTRY IN THE TRUMP SUIT, PLAN TO DRAW TRUMPS ENDING IN DUMMY. OBVIOUSLY, THE MORE TRUMPS YOU HAVE IN DUMMY THE EASIER IT IS TO END UP THERE.

(12) CAN YOU SEE IT?

Both sides vulnerable
Dealer South

North
♠ K Q 9
♡ A Q 3 2
◇ A 4
♣ A J 10 5

South
♠ A J 10 8 7 6
♡ J 5 4
◇ J 7 6
♣ K

South	West	North	East
2 ♠*	Pass	6 ♠	All Pass

*Weak Two Bid

Opening lead: ◇ 2

Your partner has given you a vote of confidence. Can you justify it? Trumps are 3-1, West having the length.

CAN YOU SEE IT? (Solution)

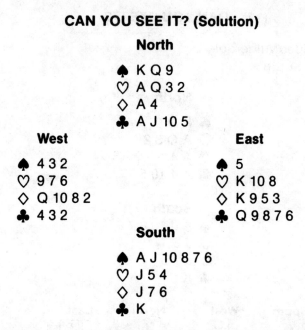

North
♠ K Q 9
♡ A Q 3 2
◇ A 4
♣ A J 10 5

West
♠ 4 3 2
♡ 9 7 6
◇ Q 10 8 2
♣ 4 3 2

East
♠ 5
♡ K 10 8
◇ K 9 5 3
♣ Q 9 8 7 6

South
♠ A J 10 8 7 6
♡ J 5 4
◇ J 7 6
♣ K

You have a diamond loser and a possible heart loser. One diamond can be ruffed in dummy, and a heart discarded on the ace of clubs. The contract would then depend upon the heart finesse. Maybe you can do better. Take a look at that club suit.

What if you rose with the ace of diamonds, cashed the king of clubs, drew three rounds of trumps ending in dummy, discarded a DIAMOND on the ace of clubs and led the jack of clubs, intending to discard another diamond if it was not covered?

If the jack of clubs is covered, ruff, enter dummy with the ACE of hearts and discard your remaining diamond on the ten of clubs. Concede a heart and score up the slam.

If the jack of clubs loses to the queen in West, you still have the ten of clubs available for one heart discard and still have the heart finesse available for your contract.

By playing clubs before hearts you avoid the heart finesse whenever the queen of clubs is in the East hand.

KEY LESSON POINTERS

1. ALWAYS BE ON THE LOOKOUT FOR LOSER ON LOSER PLAYS. (TWO OR MORE EQUALS FACING A VOID WITH ONE HIGHER CARD OUTSTANDING.)
2. BE FAMILIAR WITH THE HEART COMBINATION IN THIS HAND. IN ORDER NOT TO LOSE A HEART TRICK YOU MUST FIND WEST WITH EITHER THE SINGLETON OR DOUBLETON KING. DO NOT LEAD THE JACK. IF WEST DOES HAVE A DOUBLETON KING HE WILL COVER AND ONCE AGAIN YOU WILL HAVE A HEART LOSER.

(13) GAMBLING

North-South vulnerable
Dealer North

North
♠ 7 3
♡ 10 9
♢ A K 10 9 7 6 5
♣ 7 4

South
♠ K Q 6
♡ A J 2
♢ 4 2
♣ K Q 9 5 3

North	West	South	East
3 ♢	Pass	3 NT	All Pass

Opening lead: ♠ 4

East wins the ace and returns the ten to your king, West playing the jack.

At trick three you lead a diamond and West plays the jack. What is your plan?

GAMBLING (Solution)

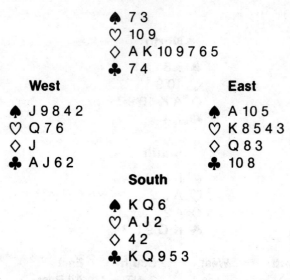

North
♠ 7 3
♡ 10 9
♢ A K 10 9 7 6 5
♣ 7 4

West
♠ J 9 8 4 2
♡ Q 7 6
♢ J
♣ A J 6 2

East
♠ A 10 5
♡ K 8 5 4 3
♢ Q 8 3
♣ 10 8

South
♠ K Q 6
♡ A J 2
♢ 4 2
♣ K Q 9 5 3

Your plan should be to DUCK the diamond. You have two sure spade tricks along with the ace of hearts. You need SIX diamond tricks, not seven. By ducking the diamond you insure your contract even if diamonds divide 3-1.

If you win the ace of diamonds you will be at the mercy of either a good club or diamond division. Incidentally, if you do win the ace, your next play should be a club not a second high diamond. You can always test the diamonds later. You need dummy's entries to lead up to your club holding in case diamonds don't behave.

To repeat, on this hand the right play is to duck the diamond, but on somewhat similar-type hands, use whatever few entries you do have to dummy to leads towards broken strength in your own hand.

KEY LESSON POINTERS

1. WHEN HOLDING TWO EQUAL HONORS, (AS IN SPADES) IT IS ALMOST ALWAYS RIGHT TO WIN WITH THE HIGHER HONOR FOR DECEPTIVE PURPOSES.
2. KNOW HOW MANY TRICKS YOU NEED FROM YOUR BEST SUIT AND PLAY THAT SUIT ACCORDINGLY.
3. ON HANDS WHERE DUMMY IS RELATIVELY WEAK, USE DUMMY'S ENTRIES TO LEAD UP TO HONOR STRENGTH IN YOUR OWN HAND.
4. WHEN A DEFENSIVE PLAYER THROWS AWAY AN HONOR UNDER ONE OF YOUR HONORS (AS WEST DID IN SPADES AT TRICK TWO) HE DENIES A HIGHER HONOR, TELLING PARTNER HIS OTHER CARDS ARE EQUAL TO THE HONOR HE HAS THROWN AWAY.

(14) NOT SO SOON

North-South vulnerable
Dealer East

North

♠ Q J 3 2
♡ 5 2
♢ K Q J 10
♣ J 7 4

South

♠ A 10 9 8 7 6
♡ K 8 4
♢ 9 7
♣ A Q

East	South	West	North
Pass	1 ♠	Pass	3 ♠*
Pass	4 ♠	All Pass	

*Limit Raise

Opening lead: J ♡

East wins the ace and shifts to the six of clubs. You try the queen but West wins the king and returns the eight of clubs. East plays the deuce and you win the ace.

How do you continue?

NOT SO SOON (Solution)

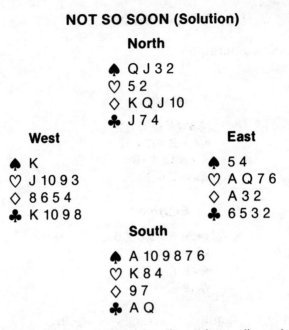

North
♠ Q J 3 2
♡ 5 2
◇ K Q J 10
♣ J 7 4

West
♠ K
♡ J 10 9 3
◇ 8 6 5 4
♣ K 10 9 8

East
♠ 5 4
♡ A Q 7 6
◇ A 3 2
♣ 6 5 3 2

South
♠ A 10 9 8 7 6
♡ K 8 4
◇ 9 7
♣ A Q

You have lost a heart and a club and must lose a diamond. The hand depends upon the location of the king of spades and the odds overwhelmingly favor a finesse with ten cards missing the king between the two hands. So?

But, you don't have to finesse spades at this very moment. Why not lead a diamond first? If someone ducks you can pitch your remaining diamond on the jack of clubs. But do not assume you are playing against relatives. Assume the diamond loses, but to whom?

If West turns up with the ace of diamonds we simply take the spade finesse but if East turns up with the ace of diamonds it is madness to take the spade finesse.

You know that East has the AQ of hearts from the opening lead. You also know that East passed originally. If East has the ace of diamonds also, he can hardly have the king of spades. No, you should play to drop the king of spades if East wins the diamond.

KEY LESSON POINTERS

1. POSTPONE FINESSES IN SUITS THAT OFFER A CHOICE OF PLAYS, (SPADES, IN THIS EXAMPLE) AS LONG AS SAFETY PERMITS.
2. LOCATING IRRELEVANT CARDS, (THE ACE OF DIAMONDS) CAN OFTEN TIMES AID YOU IN LOCATING RELEVANT ONES. (THE KING OF SPADES)
3. WHEN AN HONOR CARD IS LED, DEVELOP THE HABIT OF PLACING THE VARIOUS MISSING HONOR CARDS IN THAT SUIT.
4. A PASSED HAND IS A PASSED HAND. ONCE ONE OPPONENT HAS TURNED UP WITH NINE OR TEN HIGH CARD POINTS, THE MISSING ACES, KINGS, AND QUEENS WILL BE—GUESS WHERE?

(15) MAKE THEM PAY

Neither side vulnerable
Dealer North

North
♠ A Q 6 3 2
♡ A 10 4
♢ 10 2
♣ 6 5 3

South
♠ K J 10 8 7 5
♡ J 9 8
♢ A K 6
♣ 2

North	East	South	West
Pass	Pass	1 ♠	2 ♣
3 ♠	5 ♣	5 ♠	All Pass

Opening lead: ♣ K

West continues with the ace of clubs. Plan the play.

MAKE THEM PAY (Solution)

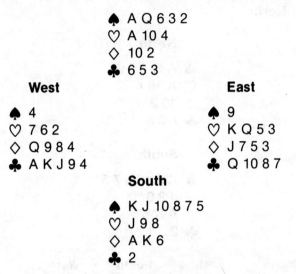

North
- ♠ A Q 6 3 2
- ♡ A 10 4
- ◇ 10 2
- ♣ 6 5 3

West
- ♠ 4
- ♡ 7 6 2
- ◇ Q 9 8 4
- ♣ A K J 9 4

East
- ♠ 9
- ♡ K Q 5 3
- ◇ J 7 5 3
- ♣ Q 10 8 7

South
- ♠ K J 10 8 7 5
- ♡ J 9 8
- ◇ A K 6
- ♣ 2

Ruff the club return, draw as many trumps as necessary and then play ace-king and ruff a diamond, stripping or eliminating that suit from both hands, ruff dummy's last club and run the jack or nine of hearts if not covered.

East will win the heart but will have to either return a heart eliminating the loser in that suit or give you a ruff-sluff with equally disastrous results.

West could have defeated the contract by shifting to a heart at trick two. It is interesting to conjecture upon which club East should play at trick one to get the heart shift he so desperately wants.

KEY LESSON POINTERS

1. WHEN YOU HAVE LOSERS IN ONLY ONE SUIT AND YOU MUST BREAK THAT SUIT FIRST, STRIP THE HAND, IF POSSIBLE, BEFORE PLAYING THAT SUIT. OF COURSE, YOU MUST LEAVE TRUMPS IN BOTH HANDS FOR THE PLAY TO WORK.
2. DO NOT BE DISCOURAGED BY THE WEAKNESS OF THE SUIT IN WHICH YOU HAVE LOSERS. EVEN A COMBINATION AS WEAK AS Jxx FACING xxx CAN MIRACULOUSLY TURN ITSELF INTO TWO LOSERS INSTEAD OF THREE IF (1) THE OPPONENT'S HOLDING IN THE SUIT IS BLOCKED (2) A DEFENSIVE ERROR IS COMMITTED.

(16) BLUNDERS

East-West vulnerable
Dealer West

North
♠ J 5
♡ 4 3
◇ Q J 7 2
♣ J 10 9 8 7

South
♠ A K Q 10 9 8 3 2
♡ K J
◇ —
♣ A K 2

West	North	East	South
Pass	Pass	4 ♡	6 ♠
All Pass			

Opening lead: ♡ Q

East wins the ace as you follow with the jack. East now lays down the ace of diamonds which you ruff with a low spade.

You cash the ace of spades and lead a low spade to the jack, East discarding a heart on the second round of spades. In dummy, you lead the jack of clubs, East plays the queen and you win and claim the balance.

How many errors, if any, in your normally impeccable play have you spotted thus far?

BLUNDERS (Solution)

North
♠ J 5
♡ 4 3
♢ Q J 7 2
♣ J 10 9 8 7

West
♠ 6 4
♡ Q
♢ K 8 6 5 4 3
♣ 6 5 4 3

East
♠ 7
♡ A 10 9 8 7 6 5 2
♢ A 10 9
♣ Q

South
♠ A K Q 10 9 8 3 2
♡ K J
♢ —
♣ A K 2

If you think everything has gone just hunky-dory so far, you are in big trouble.

You have already committed two major blunders plus a minor one, not to mention East who has committed a colossal boo boo. Let's review what has happened.

When East won the ace of hearts you should have played the king, a card you were known to hold from the lead. The jack has the same value, but it is a card that West might have from the lead.

Once you played the jack, all East had to do was return a heart for West to ruff. East KNEW you had another heart—the only outstanding heart remaining.

When East played the ace of diamonds, even though it was inconceivable that West could overruff you should have kept in shape by ruffing high. Never ruff low when you can afford to ruff high.

Finally, after cashing the ace of spades you should cash the ace of clubs before entering dummy to take the club finesse. It is just possible that West has a singleton queen of clubs. (If East were void in clubs he would have doubled six spades for an unusual lead, also if East is void in clubs you cannot make the hand.)

KEY LESSON POINTERS

1. AS DECLARER, YOU MUST PLAY ALL THE CARDS YOU ARE KNOWN TO HOLD (FROM THE OPENING LEAD AND/OR THE RETURN BY THIRD HAND) AS SOON AS POSSIBLE PROVIDING IT CANNOT COST YOU A TRICK.
2. NEVER RUFF LOW WHEN YOU CAN AFFORD TO RUFF HIGH.
3. IF YOU CAN AFFORD TO CASH A HIGH HONOR IN A SUIT BEFORE TAKING A LATER FINESSE IN THAT SUIT, DO SO.

(17)   TWO WITH TWO

Neither side vulnerable
Dealer East

                         North
                    ♠ A 8 3
                    ♡ Q J 5
                    ◇ Q 4 3 2
                    ♣ 9 6 5

                         South
                    ♠ K 7
                    ♡ K 10 9
                    ◇ K J 10 9
                    ♣ A K 10 8

East	South	West	North
2 ♠*	2 NT	Pass	3 NT
All Pass			

*Weak Two Bid (Typically a 6 card suit, 7-10 H.C.P.)

Opening lead: ♠ 5

Plan the play.

TWO WITH TWO (Solution)

North
♠ A 8 3
♡ Q J 5
◇ Q 4 3 2
♣ 9 6 5

West
♠ 5 2
♡ 8 6 4 2
◇ A 7 6
♣ J 4 3 2

East
♠ Q J 10 9 6 4
♡ A 7 3
◇ 8 5
♣ Q 7

South
♠ K 7
♡ K 10 9
◇ K J 10 9
♣ A K 10 8

At notrump contracts count your sure tricks to see how many you need to establish. On this hand you have two sure spade tricks along with two sure club tricks. You can establish three tricks in diamonds and two in hearts by driving out both aces to bring your grand total up to nine. So what's the problem?

The problem is that they have attacked your weakest suit, spades, and may be able to set up their spades before you can set up your tricks.

The general rule is: with two stoppers in their suit and two aces to drive out, hold up on the FIRST lead of their suit. This holdup play works wonders when the opposing suit is divided 6-2.

Simply follow the play on this hand if you do and do not holdup at trick one. If you win the first spade and drive out the ace of diamonds first, West wins and returns his remaining spade. East now remains with the ace of hearts and established spades. You are dead.

True, if you had knocked out the ace of hearts first you would have survived, because West would have no more spades upon gaining the lead in diamonds. But why guess?

If you win the SECOND spade, you can drive out EITHER ace first as long as East does not have both aces in which case you were always dead.

However, East would not open a weak two with a good six card suit plus two outside aces. Too strong. He would open one spade.

KEY LESSON POINTERS

1. WITH TWO STOPPERS IN YOUR WEAKEST SUIT AND TWO ACES TO DRIVE OUT, HOLD UP AND WIN THE SECOND LEAD OF THE SUIT.

(18) DOWN IS THE RIGHT ANSWER

East-West vulnerable
Dealer South

North

♠ K 10 2
♡ A K 8 7 5
♢ Q J 3
♣ 6 2

South

♠ A Q J 9 8 5
♡ 3 2
♢ 10 6 5
♣ A Q

South	West	North	East
1 ♠	Pass	2 ♡	Pass
2 ♠	Pass	4 ♠	All Pass

Opening lead: ♢ K

West continues with the ace of diamonds and a low diamond which East ruffs. East switches to the jack of clubs. Plan the play.

DOWN IS THE RIGHT ANSWER (Solution)

North
♠ K 10 2
♡ A K 8 7 5
♢ Q J 3
♣ 6 2

West
♠ 7 6
♡ 9
♢ A K 8 7 4
♣ 8 7 5 4 3

East
♠ 4 3
♡ Q J 10 6 4
♢ 9 2
♣ K J 10 9

South
♠ A Q J 9 8 5
♡ 3 2
♢ 10 6 5
♣ A Q

There are two possibilities to avoid the club loser. Take the club finesse, a 50-50 proposition, or try to set up the hearts.

In order to set up the hearts you need either a 3-3 break (36%) or a 4-2 division, (48%). Obviously it is better to work with the hearts, an 84% chance.

Allowing for the possibility of a 4-2 division you must conserve two dummy entries outside of the heart suit, one to ruff a fourth heart and one more to get over to use the fifth heart.

Proper play is to rise with the ace of clubs, cash the ace of spades and play the ace-king of hearts. Surprise! West ruffs and leads a club to East's king. You are down two and the club finesse worked all along. Why am I so mean to you? No matter. It is normal to go down two on this hand. Only someone who misplayed the hand badly would make it.

KEY LESSON POINTERS

1. WHEN ESTABLISHING A SUIT IN WHICH YOU AND YOUR PARTNER HAVE A TOTAL OF SEVEN CARDS YOU SHOULD BE FAMILIAR WITH THE PERCENTAGES OF NORMAL SUIT DIVISIONS. 3-3 = 36%, 4-2 = 48%.
2. WHEN ESTABLISHING A SIDE SUIT WHEREIN THE ONLY SIDE ENTRY (ENTRIES) TO DUMMY ARE IN THE TRUMP SUIT, YOU MUST ARRANGE TO DRAW ALL THE ADVERSE TRUMPS ENDING IN DUMMY BEFORE YOU CAN USE THE SUIT YOU HAVE ESTABLISHED. IF THIS IS NOT POSSIBLE, DO NOT BOTHER WITH THE LONG SUIT.
3. I HOPE YOU WENT DOWN ON THIS HAND. YOU DID! GOOD!

(19)   ONE FOR TWO

East-West vulnerable
Dealer East

North

♠ —
♡ A J 10 9 7 3
♢ 6 5 2
♣ A K J 2

South

♠ K 7 2
♡ K Q 8 6 2
♢ A Q 4
♣ 7 4

East	South	West	North
Pass	1 ♡	3 ♠	4 ♠
Dbl.	Pass	Pass	5 ♣
Pass	5 ♢	Pass	6 ♣
Pass	6 ♡	All Pass	

Opening lead: ♠ Q

North's 4 ♠ bid guaranteed a heart fit with a spade control. The rest of the auction was devoted to cue bidding.
Plan the play.

ONE FOR TWO (Solution)

North

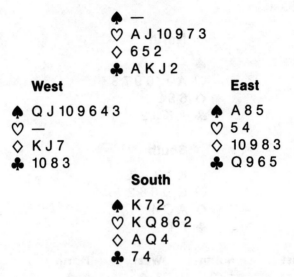

North
♠ —
♡ A J 10 9 7 3
◇ 6 5 2
♣ A K J 2

West
♠ Q J 10 9 6 4 3
♡ —
◇ K J 7
♣ 10 8 3

East
♠ A 8 5
♡ 5 4
◇ 10 9 8 3
♣ Q 9 6 5

South
♠ K 7 2
♡ K Q 8 6 2
◇ A Q 4
♣ 7 4

I hope you made East rue the day he doubled four spades. By simply discarding a diamond from dummy at trick one you insure your contract.

East wins the ace of spades and returns a diamond but you are in control. Win the ace of diamonds, draw trumps and discard dummy's remaining diamond on the spade king.

Had East not doubled, and had West led a club, the way the cards lie, the hand cannot be made against best defense.

KEY LESSON POINTERS

1. WHEN DUMMY HAS MORE TRUMPS THAN YOU, COUNT DUMMY'S LOSERS RATHER THAN YOUR OWN. IN THIS CASE DUMMY HAS TWO POSSIBLE DIAMOND LOSERS, THE TWO CLUB LOSERS CAN BE RUFFED IN THE CLOSED HAND.
2. WHEN DUMMY HAS A VOID SUIT AND THE CLOSED HAND THE KING, OR BETTER, THE KING-QUEEN, A TRICK (OR TWO) USUALLY CAN BE GAINED BY DISCARDING A LOSER FROM DUMMY. ASSUMING THE ACE WINS, YET ANOTHER LOSER CAN BE DISCARDED ON THE KING. IN THIS WAY YOU ARE EXCHANGING ONE LOSER IN THE VOID SUIT FOR TWO LOSERS IN ANOTHER SUIT. SIMILARLY WHEN DECLARER HAS QJx(x) DISCARD FROM DUMMY AND LATER TAKE A RUFFING FINESSE.

(20) DANGER!

Both sides vulnerable
Dealer South

North

♠ Q J 10 9
♡ 8 6
◇ 10 7 5 4
♣ A J 7

South

♠ A 5 3
♡ K Q 9
◇ A J 3
♣ K Q 10 9

South	West	North	East
1 ♣	Pass	1 ♠	Pass
2 NT	Pass	3 NT	All Pass

Opening lead: ♡ 3

East produces the jack of hearts. Do you win this trick? What is your plan?

DANGER! (Solution)

North

♠ Q J 10 9
♡ 8 6
♦ 10 7 5 4
♣ A J 7

West

♠ K 4
♡ A 10 4 3 2
♦ 8 6 2
♣ 6 3 2

East

♠ 8 7 6 2
♡ J 7 5
♦ K Q 9
♣ 8 5 4

South

♠ A 5 3
♡ K Q 9
♦ A J 3
♣ K Q 10 9

KQx stoppers are very similar to AJx stoppers. The main considerations should be—which opponent is apt to get the lead next?

Let's go back a bit. East's play of the jack of hearts marks the A 10 with West. (East plays third hand high unless East has equal high cards.) Therefore the play of the jack denies both the ace and the ten.

If you take the trick, West will be sitting over you with the A 10 of hearts. Therefore EAST is the danger hand. East is the one that can lead through your hearts.

However, on this hand you will be playing spades for your needed tricks and the spade finesse is headed into the West hand. West cannot hurt you by leading a second round of hearts because you still retain a stopper.

Therefore you should win the first heart with the KING, enter dummy with the jack of clubs and run the queen of spades into West. Assuming the finesse loses, you have nine tricks, three spades, four clubs, a heart and a diamond and no lead from West can hurt you.

KEY LESSON POINTERS

1. WHEN HOLDING A KQ COMBINATION, WIN THE FIRST TRICK IF THE FIRST FINESSE IS HEADED INTO YOUR LEFT HAND OPPONENT. IF IT IS HEADED INTO YOUR RIGHT HAND OPPONENT—HOLD UP!
2. WHEN YOU HOLD A KQ COMBINATION AND YOU DECIDE TO WIN THE FIRST TRICK, TAKE THE JACK WITH THE KING, NOT THE QUEEN. IF YOU WIN WITH THE KING, YOUR LEFT HAND OPPONENT CANNOT POSSIBLY TELL WHO HAS THE QUEEN. IF YOU WIN WITH THE QUEEN, YOUR LEFT HAND OPPONENT KNOWS YOU REMAIN WITH THE KING.

(21) THE OTHER WAY AROUND

Neither side vulnerable
Dealer East

North

♠ K Q J 6
♡ Q 8 5 4
♢ A 9 8
♣ A 3

South

♠ 2
♡ K J 10 9 7 6
♢ 7 3 2
♣ K J 5

East	South	West	North
1 ♢	2 ♡*	Pass	4 ♡
All Pass			

*Weak Jump Overcall

Opening lead: ♢ 6

What is your plan?

THE OTHER WAY AROUND (Solution)

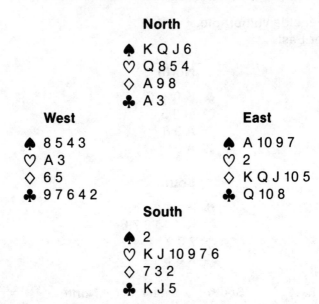

North
- ♠ K Q J 6
- ♡ Q 8 5 4
- ◇ A 9 8
- ♣ A 3

West
- ♠ 8 5 4 3
- ♡ A 3
- ◇ 6 5
- ♣ 9 7 6 4 2

East
- ♠ A 10 9 7
- ♡ 2
- ◇ K Q J 10 5
- ♣ Q 10 8

South
- ♠ 2
- ♡ K J 10 9 7 6
- ◇ 7 3 2
- ♣ K J 5

This hand can trip you up if you don't count losers.

After the ace of diamonds is removed you remain with two diamond losers, a spade, and a heart.

The problem is that the opponents have gotten off to the best lead and your spade suit in dummy is actually WORTHLESS. You can knock out the ace of spades, but what good? The opponents will simply take two diamond tricks and even you can't talk them out of the ace of trumps.

If you can't discard any diamonds from your hand on any spades in dummy, how about the other way around? How about discarding a diamond from dummy on a club winner from your hand? Yes, it does mean finessing the jack of clubs, but it is your only real chance.

Win the ace of diamonds and play ace and a club to the jack. Assuming this wins, play the king of clubs and discard a diamond loser from dummy. Now you can go about your business. You can lose no more than a spade, a heart and a diamond.

KEY LESSON POINTERS

1. THE THREE MAIN WAYS OF RIDDING YOURSELF OF LOSERS ARE: (1) RUFFING THEM IN DUMMY (2) DISCARDING THEM ON WINNERS FROM DUMMY (3) DISCARDING A LOSER FROM DUMMY UPON A WINNER FROM THE CLOSED HAND.
2. IT IS IMPORTANT TO SEE THE DIFFERENCE BETWEEN EVENTUAL AND IMMEDIATE LOSERS. ONCE DIAMONDS HAVE BEEN ATTACKED YOUR EVENTUAL DIAMOND LOSERS HAVE BECOME IMMEDIATE. HEADACHE TIME.

(22) A TALE OF TWO SUITS

Neither side vulnerable
Dealer South

North
- ♠ A J 10
- ♡ 10 3
- ◇ K 7 4 2
- ♣ 10 8 7 6

South
- ♠ 9 2
- ♡ 9
- ◇ A 8 6
- ♣ A K Q J 5 3 2

South	West	North	East
1 ♣	Pass	1 ◇	1 ♡
3 ♣	4 ♡	5 ♣	All Pass

Opening lead: ♡ 5

East wins the ace of hearts and returns the seven.

1. Just for practice, how do you place all the missing heart honors?
2. What is your game plan?

A TALE OF TWO SUITS (Solution)

North

♠ A J 10
♡ 10 3
♢ K 7 4 2
♣ 10 8 7 6

West

♠ Q 8 7 4
♡ K J 6 5
♢ Q 10 9 5
♣ 9

East

♠ K 7 5 3
♡ A Q 8 7 4 2
♢ J 3
♣ 4

South

♠ 9 2
♡ 9
♢ A 8 6
♣ A K Q J 5 3 2

As for the missing heart honors, West must have the king, (East won with the ace). As West would have led the king if he had the queen as well, it is safe to assume East has the queen. Given that East has the queen, West probably has the jack as East would probably return the queen holding ace-queen-jack.

Now back to the hand. You have lost a heart and have a spade as well as a diamond loser. Counting tricks, you have seven clubs, two diamonds and a spade for a grand total of 10. Anyway you look at it, you must find an extra trick.

You have two possible plays, (1) take two spade finesses to try to rid yourself of your diamond loser. (2) Play diamonds hoping for a 3-3 split.

As for percentages, one of two finesses is about 76%, while trying to break a suit 3-3 is 36%. Take two spade finesses.

KEY LESSON POINTERS

1. TRY TO WORK OUT THE POSITION OF THE ADVERSE HONORS IN THE SUIT THAT HAS BEEN LED FROM THE CARD THAT THIRD HAND PLAYS TO THE FIRST TRICK. IN THEORY, HE DENIES THE CARD DIRECTLY BENEATH THE ONE THAT HE PLAYS.
2. NEEDING BUT ONE OF TWO FINESSES TO SUCCEED YOU CAN COUNT ON A 76% CHANCE OF SUCCESS.
3. NEEDING A SUIT TO BREAK 3-3 WILL GIVE YOU ONLY A 36% CHANCE OF SUCCESS. THEREFORE IT STANDS TO REASON THAT GIVEN A CHOICE YOU SHOULD OPT FOR ONE OF TWO FINESSES.

(23) DISCARDS

Both sides vulnerable
Dealer South

North
♠ J 6 5 4
♡ 8 7
◇ 7 6 4 2
♣ K 7 4

South
♠ A K
♡ J 10 9
◇ A K 3
♣ A Q 10 6 2

South	West	North	East
2 NT	Pass	3 ♣*	Pass
3 ◇**	Pass	3 NT	All Pass

*Stayman
**No four card major

Opening lead: ♡ 2

The opponents reel off four heart tricks, East winding up on lead. East shifts to the jack of diamonds. What have you discarded from both hands, and how do you continue?

DISCARDS (Solution)

North

♠ J 6 5 4
♡ 8 7
♢ 7 6 4 2
♣ K 7 4

West

♠ 9 7 3 2
♡ K Q 5 2
♢ Q 9 8 5
♣ 5

East

♠ Q 10 8
♡ A 6 4 3
♢ J 10
♣ J 9 8 3

South

♠ A K
♡ J 10 9
♢ A K 3
♣ A Q 10 6 2

Keep your eye on the ball. In order to make this hand you are going to have to bring in the club suit, so don't discard any of those from EITHER hand.

From your hand you should discard your losing diamond, and from dummy a diamond and a spade, but no clubs!

Take a good look at this club suit. The proper play is to cash the ace (or queen), lead over to dummy's honor, and if West shows out, finesse the ten coming back. You can't make this play unless you keep THREE clubs on the board.

KEY LESSON POINTERS

1. BE CAREFUL WHEN DISCARDING ON OPPONENT'S WINNERS. KEEP THE SUIT THAT YOU MUST ESTABLISH FLUID ON BOTH SIDES.
2. WHEN ATTACKING A SUIT SUCH AS (AK10xx, AQ10xx, KQ10xx) FACING HONOR THIRD (Axx, Kxx, Qxx) PLAY A HIGH HONOR FROM THE LONG SIDE, THEN OVER TO THE HONOR ON THE SHORT SIDE AND FINALLY BACK TO THE HONOR ON THE LONG SIDE. IF DURING THIS LITTLE EXCURSION AN OPPONENT SHOWS OUT ON THE SECOND ROUND, YOU MAY BE ABLE TO FINESSE THE TEN ON THE RETURN TRIP.

(24) PUTTING IT TOGETHER

Both sides vulnerable
Dealer West

North
- ♠ A 6 3
- ♡ K J 5 3
- ◇ 10 9 8
- ♣ K 8 2

South
- ♠ K 10 2
- ♡ A Q 8 7 2
- ◇ 6 3
- ♣ A 9 3

West	North	East	South
1 ◇	Pass	Pass	1 ♡
1 ♠	3 ♡	Pass	4 ♡
All Pass			

Opening lead: ◇ K

West continues with the ace and queen of diamonds, East playing the four, five and seven.

You ruff and play the ace of hearts and a heart to the king, both opponents following. How do you continue?

PUTTING IT TOGETHER (Solution)

North

♠ A 6 3
♡ K J 5 3
♢ 10 9 8
♣ K 8 2

West

♠ Q J 9 8
♡ 6 4
♢ A K Q J 2
♣ 6 4

East

♠ 7 6 5
♡ 10 9
♢ 7 5 4
♣ Q J 10 7 5

South

♠ K 10 2
♡ A Q 8 7 2
♢ 6 3
♣ A 9 3

If ever things looked bad, this must be the time. There appears to be an inevitable club loser as well as an inevitable spade loser. Do not despair—there is hope!

First, go back to the bidding. West is marked with four spades (second suit) and should have five diamonds to be bidding twice, vulnerable, opposite a passing partner.

It is reasonable to assume that West has precisely 4-2-5-2 distribution. If this is the case, and West has both spade honors you can make the hand.

Cash the ace-king of clubs, stripping West of clubs, and now play ace-king and a spade, throwing West in. With nothing left, save spades and diamonds, West must surrender a ruff and a sluff allowing you to rid yourself of your club loser.

KEY LESSON POINTERS

1. USE THE BIDDING TO WORK OUT THE OPPONENT'S DISTRIBUTION.
2. GOOD PLAYERS DO NOT BID TWICE OPPOSITE A PASSING PARTNER WITHOUT A LITTLE DISTRIBUTION—PARTICULARLY VULNERABLE. ASSUME 5-4, AT LEAST, IF TWO SUITS ARE BID. IF A SUIT IS REBID, ASSUME AT LEAST SIX CARDS.
3. STRIPPING A SUIT DOES NOT ALWAYS MEAN REMOVING THE SUIT FROM BOTH YOUR HAND AND DUMMY. AS LONG AS YOU STRIP THE SUIT FROM THE PLAYER BEING THROWN IN, THAT IS GOOD ENOUGH. IN THIS CASE REMOVING BOTH OF WEST'S CLUBS ALLOWS YOU TO THROW WEST IN WITH A SPADE THUS FORCING A FAVORABLE RETURN. THIS IS AN EXAMPLE OF A PARTIAL STRIP.

(25) BE THANKFUL

East-West vulnerable
Dealer South

North
- ♠ J 8 2
- ♡ A 7 5 3 2
- ♢ 7 6 5
- ♣ K J

South
- ♠ A K Q 10 9 7 3
- ♡ 9
- ♢ A K J
- ♣ A Q

South	West	North	East
2 ♣*	Pass	2 ♡	Pass
2 ♠	Pass	3 ♠	Pass
4 NT	Pass	5 ♢	Pass
5 NT	Pass	6 ♢	Pass
7 ♠	All Pass		

*Artificial and forcing.

Opening lead: ♣ 10

Plan the play.

BE THANKFUL (Solution)

North
♠ J 8 2
♡ A 7 5 3 2
♢ 7 6 5
♣ K J

West
♠ 6 4
♡ Q J 8
♢ Q 10 9 2
♣ 10 9 8 7

East
♠ 5
♡ K 10 6 4
♢ 8 4 3
♣ 6 5 4 3 2

South
♠ A K Q 10 9 7 3
♡ 9
♢ A K J
♣ A Q

Your only possible loser is in diamonds, a suit which offers a finesse. Save finesses as last resort measures!

You have been blessed with a five card heart suit in dummy. You have a singleton heart in your own hand leaving the opponents with a total of seven hearts. If those seven hearts are divided 4-3 you can ruff THREE hearts in your hand and establish the fifth heart for a diamond discard.

You must realize that outside of the ace of hearts you are going to need THREE ADDITIONAL DUMMY ENTRIES to set up that fifth heart. Do you have them? Yes. The king of clubs plus the jack and eight of spades.

Win the ACE of clubs, cash the ace of spades and play ace of hearts and ruff a heart high. Enter dummy with the eight of spades, ruff another heart high, back to dummy with the jack of spades to ruff yet another heart. The fifth heart is now established and you can enjoy it by entering dummy with the king of clubs.

KEY LESSON POINTERS

1. A FIVE OR SIX CARD SIDE SUIT IN DUMMY IS A GIFT, DON'T ABUSE IT.
2. COUNT LOSERS AND DETERMINE HOW MANY TRICKS YOU NEED FROM YOUR LONG SUIT. IF THE SUIT CAN BE DEVELOPED, WORK ON IT AT ONCE.
3. IF YOU DO NOT HAVE THE ENTRIES, FORGET THE LONG SUIT. THERE IS ENOUGH MISERY IN THE WORLD ALREADY.
4. FINESSES IN SHORT SUITS CAN FREQUENTLY BE AVOIDED BY SETTING UP LONG SUITS. IT'S BEEN A BAD YEAR FOR FINESSES BUT A GOOD ONE FOR LONG SUITS.

(26) OOPS!

North-South vulnerable
Dealer South

North
♠ A K 8
♡ 6 4
◇ K Q 10 6 2
♣ K 8 3

South
♠ 4 2
♡ A K Q 10 5 3
◇ A J 3
♣ A 2

South	West	North	East
1 ♡	Pass	2 ◇	Pass
3 ♡	Pass	4 NT	Pass
5 ♠	Pass	5 NT	Pass
7 ♡	All Pass		

Opening lead: ♣ Q

Seven diamonds would have been easier, but why should you let your partner play an easy contract, when you can play a hard one.

You win the ace of clubs and plunk down the ace-king of hearts. The good news is that West does not have four hearts to the jack; the bad news is that East does. West discards a club on the second heart. Plan the play.

OOPS! (Solution)

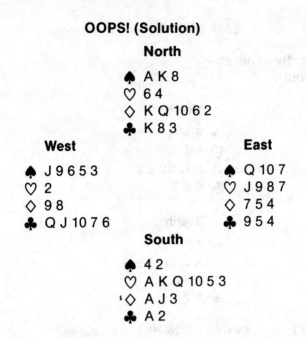

North
♠ A K 8
♡ 6 4
◇ K Q 10 6 2
♣ K 8 3

West
♠ J 9 6 5 3
♡ 2
◇ 9 8
♣ Q J 10 7 6

East
♠ Q 10 7
♡ J 9 8 7
◇ 7 5 4
♣ 9 5 4

South
♠ 4 2
♡ A K Q 10 5 3
◇ A J 3
♣ A 2

The only way to make this contract is not to lose a trick to that guarded jack of hearts in the East hand. In order to do that, you must reduce your trump holding to the same length as East plus arrange to end in DUMMY with a two card end position. Your last two cards must be the Q10 of hearts while East's will be the guarded jack. With the lead in dummy East will be rendered helpless.

In order to reduce yourself to East's size you must ruff twice in your own hand. Play the king of clubs and ruff a club, cash the ace-king of spades and ruff a spade. You remain with two trumps and three diamonds. Dummy remains with five diamonds. East is known to remain with two hearts and for your play to succeed he must have three diamonds as well. Cash three rounds of diamonds ending in dummy. When you lead a fourth diamond East must trump. You overtrump. How nice.

KEY LESSON POINTERS

1. REDUCING YOUR TRUMP HOLDING TO THE SAME LENGTH AS YOUR RIGHT HAND OPPONENT FREQUENTLY ALLOWS YOU TO PICK UP AN UNFINESSEABLE HONOR—PROVIDING YOU CAN ARRANGE TO END UP IN DUMMY WITH TWO CARDS TO BE PLAYED.
2. TRUMP REDUCTION PLAYS FREQUENTLY REQUIRE THAT THE OPPONENT WITH THE REMAINING TRUMPS HAS A RATHER BALANCED DISTRIBUTION. HOWEVER, IF IT IS YOUR ONLY CHANCE—WHAT DO YOU HAVE TO LOSE?

(27)   WHEN IT HAS TO BE

Neither side vulnerable
Dealer West

North
♠ K J
♡ 10 9 8 5 4
◇ A Q 8
♣ 9 4 3

South
♠ 10 5 3
♡ A K Q J 7
◇ 4 3
♣ A J 5

West	North	East	South
Pass	Pass	Pass	1 ♡
Dbl.	4 ♡	All Pass	

Opening lead: ♣ K

East plays the six of clubs and you allow the trick to hold, hoping that West will continue the suit. No luck, West shifts to a low spade. Which spade do you play from dummy?

WHEN IT HAS TO BE (Solution)

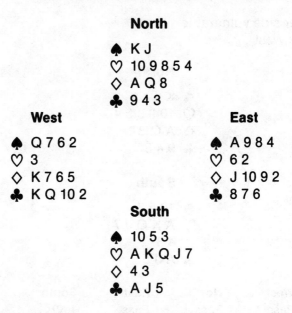

North
♠ K J
♡ 10 9 8 5 4
◇ A Q 8
♣ 9 4 3

West
♠ Q 7 6 2
♡ 3
◇ K 7 6 5
♣ K Q 10 2

East
♠ A 9 8 4
♡ 6 2
◇ J 10 9 2
♣ 8 7 6

South
♠ 10 5 3
♡ A K Q J 7
◇ 4 3
♣ A J 5

Before you "guess" which spade to play you must do a little thinking about the bidding; which high cards West has, and what you need to make this contract.

It certainly looks like you have two club losers and at least one spade loser even if you guess correctly. This means you have a minimum of three losers outside of diamonds. In other words, even though you don't know who has the king of diamonds, you need it in the West hand to make your contract. SO PUT IT THERE!

Let's see if that helps with the spade position. West has passed originally and has turned up with the K Q ♣ known and the K ◇ assumed. If he had the ace of spades as well he would have opened. He didn't, so East must have the spade ace. Play the JACK.

KEY LESSON POINTERS

1. WHEN NEEDING A PARTICULAR CARD TO BE IN A PARTICULAR HAND TO MAKE YOUR CONTRACT, ASSUME THE CARD IS WHERE YOU WANT IT TO BE. THIS MAY HELP YOU PLACE OTHER CARDS.

2. A PLAYER WHO PASSES ORIGINALLY AND THEN TURNS UP WITH 8 OR 9 HIGH CARD POINTS IN THE EARLY PLAY IS EXTREMELY UNLIKELY TO HOLD ANY MISSING ACE OR KING. ON THIS HAND WEST TURNED UP WITH FIVE POINTS IN CLUBS (KNOWN) AND THREE POINTS IN DIAMONDS (POSITIVELY ASSUMED) THEREFORE WEST COULD NOT LOGICALLY OWN THE ACE OF SPADES.

(28) BETTER SAFE THAN SORRY

Both sides vulnerable
Dealer South

North
♠ K 8 3
♡ Q 10 5 3
◇ A Q J 10 5
♣ A

South
♠ 7
♡ A K J 9 8 7 4 2
◇ 3 2
♣ 6 5

South	West	North	East
4 ♡	Pass	4 NT	Pass
5 ◇	Pass	6 ♡	All Pass

Opening lead: ♣ K

East plays the four. Plan the play.

BETTER SAFE THAN SORRY (Solution)

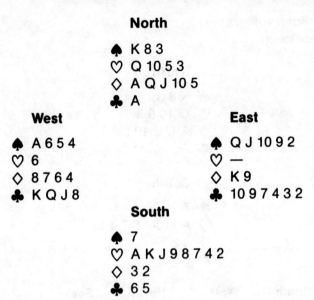

North

♠ K 8 3
♡ Q 10 5 3
◇ A Q J 10 5
♣ A

West

♠ A 6 5 4
♡ 6
◇ 8 7 6 4
♣ K Q J 8

East

♠ Q J 10 9 2
♡ —
◇ K 9
♣ 10 9 7 4 3 2

South

♠ 7
♡ A K J 9 8 7 4 2
◇ 3 2
♣ 6 5

You have a spade loser and a possible diamond loser. If you take the diamond finesse and it works you make an overtrick. Congratulations. But if it loses they cash a spade and you go down one. In other words finessing the diamond is a 50-50 proposition.

However, if you lead a SPADE toward the king BEFORE taking the diamond finesse you double your chances of making the slam!

You make the hand if West has EITHER the ace of spades or the king of diamonds. Assuming West wins the ace of spades (best), you have a parking place for your losing diamond on the king of spades.

If the king of spades loses to East, fall back on the diamond finesse as a last resort. Two finesses are better than one.

KEY LESSON POINTERS

1. WHEN TWO FINESSES ARE AVAILABLE, EITHER OF WHICH WILL GIVE YOU YOUR CONTRACT, TAKE THE ONE THAT ALLOWS YOU TO TAKE THE OTHER IF THE FIRST ONE FAILS. TRANSLATED, THIS MEANS LEADING A SINGLETON TOWARD A KING, A KING-QUEEN OR A KING-JACK COMBINATION BEFORE TAKING ANOTHER FINESSE.

(29) A GOOD SLAM

East-West vulnerable
Dealer South

North
♠ 6 4
♡ A 10 8 3
♢ 7 4
♣ K J 10 9 6

South
♠ A K Q J 10 3
♡ Q J 4
♢ A 6
♣ A 5

South	West	North	East
2 ♣*	Pass	3 ♣	Pass
3 ♠	Pass	4 ♡	Pass
4 NT	Pass	5 ♢	Pass
5 NT	Pass	6 ♢	Pass
6 ♠	All Pass		

*Strong and artificial

Opening lead: ♢ K

Plan the play.

A GOOD SLAM (Solution)

North

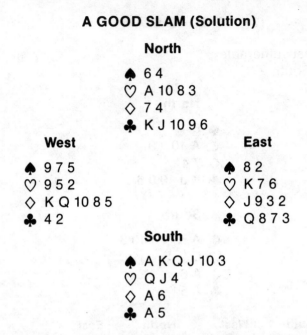

♠ 6 4
♡ A 10 8 3
♢ 7 4
♣ K J 10 9 6

West

♠ 9 7 5
♡ 9 5 2
♢ K Q 10 8 5
♣ 4 2

East

♠ 8 2
♡ K 7 6
♢ J 9 3 2
♣ Q 8 7 3

South

♠ A K Q J 10 3
♡ Q J 4
♢ A 6
♣ A 5

You have a diamond loser and a possible heart loser. If the heart finesse works you cannot lose the slam and you might make an overtrick. Let's turn our attention to clubs for a moment, dummy's length—the most common source of extra tricks.

You could play ace-king and trump a club hoping the queen drops and then take the heart finesse if it doesn't. This is surely better than simply taking the heart finesse.

However even that isn't completely safe. The queen of clubs may not drop and the heart finesse may lose. Examine the club suit a bit more closely.

Assume you win the opening lead, then draw trumps, discarding a diamond from dummy, and play the ace-king of clubs. Dummy remains with the ♣ J 10 9. These are all equal cards and only the queen is outstanding. Lead the jack of clubs and if it is not covered, discard a diamond. What can happen?

If the jack holds, the most you can lose is a heart even if the heart finesse loses. If the jack of clubs loses to the queen you still have the ten and nine to furnish heart discards.

KEY LESSON POINTERS

1. THE GREATEST SOURCE OF EXTRA TRICKS FOR DECLARER IS DUMMY'S LONG SUIT.
2. WHEN A LONG SUIT OFFERS EITHER A SIMPLE FINESSE OR A TRUMP FINESSE (WHAT YOU DID IN CLUBS ON THIS HAND) KEEP IN MIND THAT THE TRUMP FINESSE MAY ALLOW YOU TO RID YOURSELF OF AN IMMEDIATE LOSER WITHOUT PUTTING YOUR CONTRACT IN DANGER. A LOSING CLUB FINESSE WOULD HAVE ALLOWED THE OPPONENTS TO CASH A DIAMOND TRICK—THE TRUMP FINESSE DID NOT.

(30)   A GOOD GRAND

North-South vulnerable
Dealer South

North
- ♠ Q 9 5 4
- ♡ Q J 7 6
- ◇ A 8 3
- ♣ J 5

South
- ♠ A K 8 3 2
- ♡ —
- ◇ K Q 10 4
- ♣ A K Q 10

South	West	North	East
2 ♣	Pass	2 ◇	Pass
2 ♠	Pass	3 ♠	Pass
4 ♣	Pass	4 ◇	Pass
5 NT	Pass	6 ♣	Pass
6 ◇	Pass	7 ♠	All Pass

Opening lead: ♡ A

Don't worry about the bidding. Two clubs was an artificial force, two diamonds was a waiting response. The two following spades bids were natural and the next two bids were cue bids. The leap to 5 NT asked for trump honors. The six club response announced the queen or less. Six diamonds asked about the queen of spades and seven spades said, "Yes, I've got the damn thing".

Now that you are here, how do you play after ruffing the opening lead?

A GOOD GRAND (Solution)

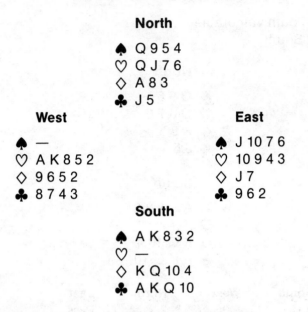

North

♠ Q 9 5 4
♡ Q J 7 6
♦ A 8 3
♣ J 5

West

♠ —
♡ A K 8 5 2
♦ 9 6 5 2
♣ 8 7 4 3

East

♠ J 10 7 6
♡ 10 9 4 3
♦ J 7
♣ 9 6 2

South

♠ A K 8 3 2
♡ —
♦ K Q 10 4
♣ A K Q 10

You should see at a glance that there is no problem unless the spades are 4-0. Even with a 3-1 division, you will be able to ruff your fourth diamond in dummy, if necessary.

Given your combined spade holding, you cannot pick up the missing spades if they are all in the West hand, but you can if they are with East. Therefore, assume they are with East, otherwise no problem.

At trick two lead a LOW spade to the queen. If everyone follows, draw trumps and claim. If West shows out, play a second spade from dummy covering East's ten with the king. Now reenter dummy with a CLUB and finesse East out of his remaining two spades.

Now all you have to worry about is the jack of diamonds. Best play is simply to run the clubs and reduce your hand to four diamonds, dummy keeping three diamonds and a heart.

Play the king of diamonds, a diamond to the ace, and if the jack hasn't dropped, play a third diamond towards your queen-ten. On this hand the jack has already dropped but if it has not, and East follows with a low diamond, a great player like you will know which one to play. Right? Of course, right.

KEY LESSON POINTERS

1. WHEN A CONTRACT LOOKS GOOD ASSUME BAD BREAKS IN KEY SUITS.
2. WHEN AN OPPONENT LEADS AN ACE AGAINST A GRAND SLAM DO NOT ASSUME THAT HIS PARTNER HOLDS THE KING. A GOOD PLAYER REALIZES THAT THE ACE MAY BE TRUMPED AND WILL BE RELUCTANT TO LEAD ONE WITHOUT THE KING.

(31) ROUTINE

East-West vulnerable
Dealer South

North
- ♠ Q J 10
- ♡ 6 5 2
- ◇ Q J 10 7 6
- ♣ 4 3

South
- ♠ K 5 4
- ♡ A K 8
- ◇ K 9 3
- ♣ A K J 5

South	West	North	East
2 NT*	Pass	3 NT	All Pass

*20-21

Opening lead: ♠ 3   East plays the ♠ 7

Plan the play.

ROUTINE (Solution)

North
- ♠ Q J 10
- ♡ 6 5 2
- ◇ Q J 10 7 6
- ♣ 4 3

West
- ♠ A 9 8 3 2
- ♡ J 9 4
- ◇ 8 2
- ♣ Q J 5

East
- ♠ 7 6
- ♡ Q 10 7 3
- ◇ A 5 4
- ♣ 10 9 8 6

South
- ♠ K 5 4
- ♡ A K 8
- ◇ K 9 3
- ♣ A K 7 2

The problem here is to recognize the problem. You would like to establish your diamonds but you must count on the possibility of an opponent winning the THIRD round of the suit.

If that turns out to be the case, it would be agreeable to have an entry to the remaining diamonds. The only possible suit in which you can develop that entry is spades. Therefore you must win the KING of spades at trick one to insure a later spade entry. Do this and you will have no trouble winning at least 10 tricks. Win the first spade cheaply and you will have trouble getting to nine!

East will win the third diamond and return a spade. If you play the king. West will allow you to hold the trick, and if you play low West will win and return a spade locking you in your hand forevermore.

KEY LESSON POINTERS

1. WHEN PLANNING TO DEVELOP A LONG SUIT IN A RELATIVELY WEAK HAND YOU MUST PROVIDE FOR A LATER ENTRY TO THAT HAND. IN SOME CASES THIS MEANS WINNING THE OPENING LEAD WITH A HIGHER CARD THAN NECESSARY TO CREATE A LATER ENTRY. FOR EXAMPLE, IF YOU HAD STARTED WITH Axx INSTEAD OF Kxx OF SPADES, YOU MUST WIN THE FIRST TRICK WITH THE ACE.
2. IF YOU PLAY TOO QUICKLY TO THE FIRST TRICK WITHOUT PLANNING, YOU WILL FREQUENTLY WIND UP WITH A VERY UNHAPPY PARTNER— BUT VERY HAPPY OPPONENTS.

(32) TWO LEADS

Neither side vulnerable
Dealer North

North
- ♠ Q
- ♡ 8 4 3
- ◇ A K Q J 9 8
- ♣ 8 7 4

South
- ♠ A 8 7 3
- ♡ A K Q 7
- ◇ 6 5
- ♣ A K 3

North	East	South	West
1 ◇	Pass	1 ♡	Pass
2 ◇	Pass	3 ♣	Pass
3 ♡	Pass	6 ♡!	All Pass

Opening lead: ♠ J

It must be late because you normally bid much better than this. East covers the queen with the king. Let's hope it is not too late for you to find the winning play.

How would you play this hand if the other black jack was led, the jack of clubs?

TWO LEADS (Solution)

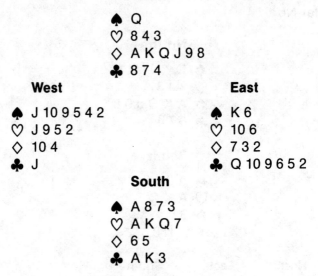

North
- ♠ Q
- ♡ 8 4 3
- ◇ A K Q J 9 8
- ♣ 8 7 4

West
- ♠ J 10 9 5 4 2
- ♡ J 9 5 2
- ◇ 10 4
- ♣ J

East
- ♠ K 6
- ♡ 10 6
- ◇ 7 3 2
- ♣ Q 10 9 6 5 2

South
- ♠ A 8 7 3
- ♡ A K Q 7
- ◇ 6 5
- ♣ A K 3

In order to run the diamond suit, a solid suit that has NO outside entry, you must be able to draw trumps—all of the trumps.

With a club lead this is no problem. Simply win the opening lead and play out the three high trumps. If they don't break 3-3, but rather 4-2, concede the trump trick and play the hand at notrump. You do have 12 notrump tricks. One spade, two clubs, three hearts and six diamonds.

Unfortunately, with a spade lead you do not have the luxury of this play. If the trumps do not break and you give up a trump trick the opponents can cash their spade winners. If, instead of giving up a trump, you begin to run diamonds, somebody ruffs and you are stuck with your black suit losers. If you try to ruff two spades in dummy you might be overruffed or run into other troubles.

No, the technique with a spade lead is to concede your probable trump loser at trick two. Lead a low trump! What can they do?

You can win any return, draw the remaining trumps, and then run the diamonds. Notice you could not safely make this play with a singleton diamond in your hand. The defense could shift to a diamond upon winning the trump trick, defeating your purpose.

KEY LESSON POINTERS

1. RUNNING A SOLID SIDE SUIT AT A SUIT CONTRACT MAY REQUIRE SPECIAL HANDLING. IF THE HAND CAN BE PLAYED AT NO TRUMP—DO IT! IF IT CANNOT, DUCKING AN EARLY ROUND OF TRUMPS MAY BE THE ANSWER.

(33) LOOKING AHEAD

East-West vulnerable
Dealer East

North
♠ 9 4
♡ K 7 6 5
♢ A Q J 10
♣ K 10 9

South
♠ A J
♡ A Q 10 9 8 4
♢ 7 6 3
♣ 7 2

East	South	West	North
1 ♠	2 ♡	2 ♠	4 ♡
All Pass			

Opening lead: ♠ 2

East plays the king. Plan the play.

LOOKING AHEAD (Solution)

North

- ♠ 9 4
- ♡ K 7 6 5
- ◇ A Q J 10
- ♣ K 10 9

West

- ♠ Q 8 6 2
- ♡ 3
- ◇ 9 5 4 2
- ♣ Q 8 6 5

East

- ♠ K 10 7 5 3
- ♡ J 2
- ◇ K 8
- ♣ A J 4 3

South

- ♠ A J
- ♡ A Q 10 9 8 4
- ◇ 7 6 3
- ♣ 7 2

You have four possible losers, one spade, one diamond and two clubs. The good news is that you can dispose of one of those losers on dummy's fourth diamond. The bad news is that the opponents may cash four tricks before you are able to do this.

The good news is that you can prevent this. The bad news is that you may not know how. The good news is that I am going to tell you. The bad news is you might forget.

You must assume the diamond finesse is going to lose because East needs the king of diamonds for his opening bid.

You must also assume that East has the ace of clubs for the same reason. What can you do?

You can prevent West, the danger hand, (because he can lead a club through your king) from ever getting the lead. What is his entry? The queen of spades. East did play the king denying the queen at trick one, remember?

By simply ducking the opening lead, you shut West out of the proceedings. You win the spade return, draw trumps and take a losing diamond finesse. East wins, but you lose one club trick instead of the two you would have lost had you won the opening lead.

KEY LESSON POINTERS

1. AFTER COUNTING LOSERS, TRY TO PLACE THEIR HONOR CARDS FROM THE BIDDING AND OPENING LEAD.
2. AVOID PUTTING AN UNPROTECTED HONOR UP FOR GRABS BY PREVENTING THE DANGER HAND FROM LEADING THROUGH THE HONOR.

(34) BUT THEY'VE TOLD YOU

North-South vulnerable
Dealer West

North

♠ A K 8 6
♡ 10 3
♢ Q J 4 2
♣ 10 4 2

South

♠ Q 2
♡ A K J 9 8 7
♢ K 5
♣ 9 5 3

West	North	East	South
1 ♣	Pass	Pass	2 ♡*
Pass	3 ♡	All Pass	

*Intermediate Jump Overcall in the Passout Seat.

Opening lead: ♣ K

West cashes three top clubs, East discarding the seven of diamonds on the third club. West shifts to the ten of diamonds, you play low from dummy and unblock the king under East's ace. East continues with a diamond won by dummy's jack.

What is the percentage play in hearts considering the suit in isolation? Plan the play.

BUT, THEY'VE TOLD YOU (Solution)

North

♠ A K 8 6
♡ 10 3
◇ Q J 4 2
♣ 10 4 2

West

♠ J 10 7
♡ Q 4
◇ 10 9 8
♣ A K Q J 6

East

♠ 9 5 4 3
♡ 5 4 2
◇ A 7 6 3
♣ 8 7

South

♠ Q 2
♡ A K J 9 8 7
◇ K 5
♣ 9 5 3

With no other guide, the proper play in hearts is to run the ten immediately, catering to Qxx or Qxxx in the East hand. It is a grave error to cash the ace first and then finesse because if East does have Qxxx you can no longer pick it up.

However, this heart suit must not be considered in isolation. It must be considered in relation to the bidding you have heard. East was unable to keep a one club bid open and has already shown up with the ace of diamonds. Had he the queen of hearts as well, he would have had six high card points and would have dug up some response.

Well, if East doesn't have the queen of hearts, two guesses as to who does. Simply plunk down the A K of hearts in hopes the queen will drop from West.

KEY LESSON POINTERS

1. AN EXPERIENCED PLAYER REALIZES THAT THE BEST PERCENTAGE PLAY FOR A PARTICULAR COMBINATION OF CARDS MAY VARY WITH THE CIRCUMSTANCES. WHEN THERE ARE ABSOLUTELY NO CLUES AVAILABLE, SIMPLY TAKE THE PERCENTAGE PLAY AND LET IT GO AT THAT.
2. WHEN A PLAYER CANNOT RESPOND TO AN OPENING ONE BID HE SHOULD BE ASSUMED TO HAVE LESS THAN 6 HIGH CARD POINTS. IF HE TURNS UP WITH AN ACE EARLY ON, HE SHOULD NOT HAVE ANY OTHER KING OR QUEEN. IF HE TURNS UP WITH A KING HE CERTAINLY WON'T HAVE ANOTHER ACE OR KING AND IS UNLIKELY TO HAVE A SIDE QUEEN. IF HE TURNS UP WITH A QUEEN AND A JACK HE SHOULD NOT HAVE ANY OTHER ACE OR KING.

(35) IS HE KIDDING ME?

Neither side vulnerable
Dealer South

North

♠ A 10 5 4
♡ 4 3
◇ A J 9 2
♣ 7 5 4

South

♠ K 6 3 2
♡ K Q
◇ K Q 10 4
♣ A 9 3

South	West	North	East
1 NT	Pass	2 ♣	Pass
2 ♠	Pass	4 ♠	All Pass

Opening lead: ♡ J

East wins the ace and fires back the queen of clubs which you allow to hold, West playing the eight. East continues with the ten of clubs which you win, West playing the six.

At trick four you plunk down the king of spades, West playing the seven and East the queen. When you lead a low spade at trick five West plays the eight. Which spade do you play from dummy?

IS HE KIDDING ME? (Solution)

North
♠ A 10 5 4
♡ 4 3
♢ A J 9 2
♣ 7 5 4

West
♠ 9 8 7
♡ J 10 8 2
♢ 8 7 6
♣ K 8 6

East
♠ Q J
♡ A 9 7 6 5
♢ 5 3
♣ Q J 10 2

South
♠ K 6 3 2
♡ K Q
♢ K Q 10 4
♣ A 9 3

You really have no choice here. As you are doomed to lose yet another club you cannot make the hand unless the QJ of spades are doubleton. Even if you finesse the ten and East shows out you still have a spade loser, so what is the point of the finesse?

KEY LESSON POINTERS

1. WHEN YOU HAVE A CHOICE OF PLAYS, ONE OF WHICH ALLOWS YOU TO MAKE THE CONTRACT IF IT WORKS, WHILE THE OTHER DOESN'T, EVEN IF IT WORKS, YOU REALLY HAVE NO CHOICE.
2. THINK POSITIVELY! PLAY TO MAKE, NOT TO GO DOWN!

(36) AGGRESSIVE BIDDING

Both sides vulnerable
Dealer West

North

♠ A 8 6 5
♡ 9 8 7 6
♢ J 10 5
♣ K 8

South

♠ K Q J 3 2
♡ A J 10
♢ 6 4
♣ A 7 5

West	North	East	South
1 ♢	Pass	Pass	Dbl.
Pass	1 ♡	Pass	1 ♠
Pass	2 ♠	Pass	3 ♠
Pass	4 ♠	All Pass	

Opening lead: ♢ K

Now that you have crawled into this game, you need only make it. West continues with the ace and queen of diamonds, East playing up the line. You ruff the third diamond and play the king-queen of spades, West discarding a diamond on the second spade. How do you continue?

AGGRESSIVE BIDDING (Solution)

North

♠ A 8 6 5
♡ 9 8 7 6
◇ J 10 5
♣ K 8

West

♠ 9
♡ K Q 4
◇ A K Q 8 3
♣ 10 9 4 2

East

♠ 10 7 3
♡ 5 3 2
◇ 9 7 2
♣ Q J 6 3

South

♠ K Q J 3 2
♡ A J 10
◇ 6 4
♣ A 7 5

You have lost two tricks and your only other losers are in hearts. There is a likelihood from the bidding that West has both heart honors. What to do?

If you draw the last trump and strip the clubs before leading a heart it will do you no good. There will be no trump in the dummy! West simply wins the heart and exits with either a diamond or a club forcing you to ruff and you won't even have a dummy reentry to finesse the heart again—just in case the honors are divided.

No, the answer is a PARTIAL STRIP. You don't necessarily have to draw all of the trumps before endplaying somebody.

After cashing two high spades, play king-ace and ruff a club. Now lead a low heart to the jack. West wins but what can he do? A heart return goes into your A 10. A minor suit return allows you to ruff with the ace of trumps (better than having a low trump in dummy, East could overtrump) and discard the ten of hearts from your hand. How your partners must worship you.

KEY LESSON POINTERS

1. SOME HANDS CANNOT BE STRIPPED ENTIRELY. IT IS STILL POSSIBLE TO EFFECT A STRIP AND END PLAY WITHOUT DRAWING ALL OF THE TRUMPS. THIS IS ANOTHER EXAMPLE OF A "PARTIAL STRIP". (See hand #24)
2. IF THE PLAYER BEING THROWN IN DOES NOT HAVE ANY TRUMP EXIT CARDS, STRIP AND END PLAYS CAN STILL WORK.

(37) ONLY NINE

East-West vulnerable
Dealer South

North
♠ K Q J 9
♡ 10 2
♢ K J 4 3
♣ 7 6 5

South
♠ 10
♡ K Q 6
♢ A 10 9 8
♣ A K J 9 2

South	West	North	East
1 ♣	Pass	1 ♠	Pass
2 ♢	Pass	3 ♢	Pass
3 NT	All Pass		

Opening lead: ♡ 4

You try the ten from dummy which holds, East playing the five.
What is your plan?

ONLY NINE (Solution)

North

♠ K Q J 9
♡ 10 2
◇ K J 4 3
♣ 7 6 5

West

♠ 8 6 4
♡ A J 8 4 3
◇ 2
♣ Q 10 8 3

East

♠ A 7 5 3 2
♡ 9 7 5
◇ Q 7 6 5
♣ 4

South

♠ 10
♡ K Q 6
◇ A 10 9 8
♣ A K J 9 2

Counting sure tricks you have two clubs, two diamonds, plus the heart you have already won for five.

You have a choice of developing any one of three suits keeping in mind you only have one heart stopper remaining.

Because you have an eventual sure trick in hearts, (their best suit) you need to develop three additional tricks.

Clearly spades is the safest suit to attack. Your first play should be the KING of spades from dummy. If it holds, continue with a second and even a third spade if necessary. It is the surest and safest route to nine tricks.

KEY LESSON POINTERS

1. MAKE SURE YOU KNOW HOW MANY ADDITIONAL TRICKS YOU NEED WHEN FACED WITH A CHOICE OF DEVELOPING ONE OF A NUMBER OF SUITS.

2. IN GENERAL TRY TO WORK WITH SUITS THAT ARE MISSING CARDS THAT HAVE TO BE LOST IN ANY EVENT. FOR EXAMPLE, IN THIS HAND THE ACE OF SPADES IS A CERTAIN LOSER. IF YOU WORK WITH CLUBS AND/OR DIAMONDS YOU MIGHT LOSE TO THE QUEEN AND STILL HAVE THE SPADE LOSER.

3. WHEN HOLDING 10x IN THE DUMMY FACING AKx, AQx or KQx BE SURE TO PLAY THE TEN WHEN A SMALL CARD IS LED. HOWEVER, HOLDING AJx, PLAY SMALL FROM DUMMY AS YOU ARE ASSURED OF TWO TRICKS IF YOU DO.

(38) UNBID SUITS

Neither side vulnerable
Dealer West

North

♠ A 3 2
♡ 6 5 4
♢ Q 10 8 6
♣ K 9 2

South

♠ K 8
♡ A 8 3
♢ 5 4 3
♣ A J 10 8 7

West	North	East	South
1 ♢	Pass	1 ♡	2 ♣
2 ♡	3 ♣	All Pass	

Opening lead: ♢ K

West continues with the ace of diamonds upon which East discards a small spade. When West plays a third diamond, you insert the ten which East ruffs. East returns the queen of hearts. Plan the play.

UNBID SUITS (Solution)

North

♠ A 3 2
♡ 6 5 4
♢ Q 10 8 6
♣ K 9 2

West

♠ Q 10 7 4
♡ K 7 2
♢ A K J 9 2
♣ 3

East

♠ J 9 6 5
♡ Q J 10 9
♢ 7
♣ Q 6 5 4

South

♠ K 8
♡ A 8 3
♢ 5 4 3
♣ A J 10 8 7

At this moment you have one heart loser (one can go on the queen of diamonds) and a trump problem. What do you know?

You know that West started with five diamonds. You know that East bid hearts and West supported hearts. You have six hearts between your hand and dummy so East must have four hearts and West three.

What about the distribution of the spade suit, the key to this hand? You have five spades between your hand and dummy, leaving East-West with eight spades. Eight spades and they were not bid! They must be 4-4. If either opponent had five spades the suit would have been mentioned. West would have opened one spade with five spades and five diamonds; East would have responded one spade in preference to one heart with five spades. Spades are 4-4. You now know the club distribution!

West started life with four spades (inferred) three hearts (assumed) and five diamonds (known). That leaves West with one club.

Win the ace of hearts, lead the jack of clubs to the king and run the nine of clubs. After trumps are drawn, enter dummy with the ace of spades and discard one losing heart on the queen of diamonds.

KEY LESSON POINTERS

1. WHEN ONE PLAYER BIDS A SUIT AND THE OTHER SUPPORTS AND YOU HAVE SIX CARDS IN THAT SUIT BETWEEN YOUR HAND AND DUMMY, ASSUME THE SUIT IS DIVIDED 4-3.
2. IF BOTH OPPONENTS BID AND DO NOT SO MUCH AS MENTION A MAJOR SUIT IN WHICH YOU HAVE FIVE CARDS BETWEEN YOUR HAND AND DUMMY, ASSUME THE SUIT IS DIVIDED 4-4.

(39) FLIM FLAM

East-West vulnerable
Dealer South

North
♠ 7 6
♡ A K Q J
♢ Q J 7
♣ J 9 8 7

South
♠ K Q 5
♡ 7 2
♢ A 10 9 4 2
♣ K 6 2

South	West	North	East
1 ♢	Pass	1 ♡	Pass
1 NT	Pass	3 NT	All Pass

Opening lead: ♠ 4   East plays the Jack.

Plan the play.

FLIM FLAM (Solution)

North
♠ 7 6
♡ A K Q J
◇ Q J 7
♣ J 9 8 7

West	East
♠ A 10 8 4 2	♠ J 9 3
♡ 8 6 5	♡ 10 9 4 3
◇ K 6	◇ 8 5 3
♣ 10 5 3	♣ A Q 4

South
♠ K Q 5
♡ 7 2
◇ A 10 9 4 2
♣ K 6 2

You have four top heart tricks as well as one spade trick. You are going to have to establish diamonds. The diamond finesse is going into the West hand so you should win the first spade, retaining a second stopper in the suit.

However, you must win the spade with the KING. If you win with the queen, West will know from his partner's play of the jack, (third hand high unless holding equal high cards) that you remain with the king.

If West knows you still have the king, he may switch to a club upon winning the king of diamonds. This will result in a two trick set. If, however, you win with the king, West may think his partner has the queen. If he does, he will continue spades upon winning the king of diamonds. You now make an overtrick.

KEY LESSON POINTERS

1. WHEN HOLDING TWO CARDS OF EQUAL VALUE IT GENERALLY PAYS FOR THE DECLARER TO WIN THE TRICK WITH THE HIGHER EQUAL. A MAJOR EXCEPTION (ONE OF THE FEW) IS WHEN HOLDING THE A K OF A SUIT AT NOTRUMP. IN THAT CASE, WIN THE FIRST TRICK WITH THE KING. IF YOU WIN WITH THE ACE, THE OPPONENTS MAY BECOME SUSPICIOUS WONDERING WHY YOU DID NOT HOLD UP IF THAT WAS YOUR ONLY STOPPER.

2. BY UNDERSTANDING THIRD HAND PLAY, YOU WILL UNDERSTAND THE EFFECTS OF YOUR PLAYS ON THE OPENING LEADER.

3. CONCEAL SMALL CARDS EARLY IN THE PLAY IT CONFUSES THE OPPONENT'S COUNT. FOR EXAMPLE, PLAY THE FOUR OF DIAMONDS, NOT THE DEUCE, UNDER THE QUEEN WHEN FINESSING DIAMONDS.

(40)   TRADE OFF

Both sides vulnerable
Dealer North

North
♠ K J 9
♡ A 5
♢ 5 4 2
♣ A K 7 5 4

South
♠ A Q 10 7 5 4
♡ 3
♢ K 6 3
♣ 6 3 2

North	East	South	West
1 ♣	Pass	1 ♠	2 ♡
2 ♠	3 ♡	4 ♠	All Pass

Opening lead: ♡ K

What is your plan of play?

TRADE OFF (Solution)

North
♠ K J 9
♡ A 5
◊ 5 4 2
♣ A K 7 5 4

West
♠ 3 2
♡ K Q 9 8 7 6
◊ A 8 7
♣ 10 9

East
♠ 8 6
♡ J 10 4 2
◊ Q J 10 9
♣ Q J 8

South
♠ A Q 10 7 5 4
♡ 3
◊ K 6 3
♣ 6 3 2

You have four losers, one club and three possible diamond losers. As always, try to set up the long suit, clubs, in order to discard the losers from the evenly divided suit, diamonds.

As usual, the problem is that upon winning a trick in clubs, the wrong defender (East) may have the lead and may shoot a diamond through your king. If you lose three diamond tricks, the good clubs in dummy go down the drain.

You must set up the clubs without letting East in. How? Exchange a loser. Let West hold the opening lead! True, you had no heart loser originally and you have just created one—but now you have no club loser because the ace of hearts can be used to discard a club. The difference is that West (the non-danger hand) has the lead. In the other case East would have had the lead.

West is helpless when allowed to hold the king of hearts. He really can do more than continue a heart. You discard a club, Cash the ace of clubs, enter your hand with a spade and lead a second club towards the king. (In case West has a singleton club—let him ruff air.) When the king holds, ruff a club high, draw trumps ending in dummy and discard two diamonds on the established clubs. Making five.

KEY LESSON POINTERS

1. THE KEY TO THE PLAY OF MOST HANDS IS ESTABLISHING THE LONG SUIT IN DUMMY IN ORDER TO DISPOSE OF LOSERS IN SHORTER SUITS.
2. EVERY SO OFTEN THE DANGER HAND THEME CROPS UP—AN ENEMY HAND YOU DO NOT WANT TO HAVE THE LEAD—IF YOU CAN TRANSFER A LOSER FROM THE DANGER TO THE NON-DANGER HAND—DO IT!

(41) EVEN IT OUT

North-South vulnerable
Dealer North

North

♠ 8 6 5
♡ A 5 3 2
◇ K Q 7 5
♣ Q J

South

♠ A 4
♡ K J 10
◇ A 10 9 8 6
♣ A K 3

North	East	South	West
Pass	Pass	1 ◇	Pass
1 ♡	Pass	2 NT	Pass
4 ◇	Pass	6 ◇	All Pass

Opening lead: ♠ J

Trumps are 2-2. Plan the play.

EVEN IT OUT (Solution)

North

♠ 8 6 5
♡ A 5 3 2
♢ K Q 7 5
♣ Q J

West	East
♠ J 10 9 7	♠ K Q 3 2
♡ Q 9 7	♡ 8 6 4
♢ 3 2	♢ J 4
♣ 9 8 4 2	♣ 10 7 6 5

South

♠ A 4
♡ K J 10
♢ A 10 9 8 6
♣ A K 3

You have a certain spade loser and a possible heart loser. If you finesse hearts and it loses, the opponents will cash their spade trick.

Hands that have losers in TWO suits, one of which is inevitable (spades) and one which is not, (hearts) lend themselves to strip and throw-in plays.

The trick is to give up the spade trick at such a time that ANY return costs the defenders a trick. In order to do this you must (1) remove all their safe exit cards (2) throw them in with a suit that is equally divided between your hand and dummy.

The play here is to win the opening lead, draw trumps, and play three rounds of clubs discarding a SPADE from the table. That discard of the spade is the key play of the hand. It now evens out the spade holding between your hand and dummy. Now when you concede a spade, the opponents cannot safely play a third spade as that would give you a ruff and a sluff. They have to broach hearts. Once a heart is led from either side, your possible heart loser is eliminated.

KEY LESSON POINTERS

1. WITH LOSERS IN TWO SUITS TRY TO THROW THE OPPONENTS IN WITH ONE OF THOSE SUITS IN ORDER TO FORCE A LEAD IN THE OTHER.
2. IN ORDER TO FORCE A LEAD IN A SUIT YOU WANT LED, YOU MUST STRIP THE OPPONENTS OF ALL SAFE EXIT CARDS, LEAVE TRUMPS ON BOTH SIDES, AND TRY TO THROW THEM IN WITH A SUIT THAT IS EVENLY DIVIDED BETWEEN YOUR HAND AND DUMMY.
3. IF NO SUIT IS EVENLY DIVIDED BETWEEN YOUR HAND AND DUMMY, ARRANGE TO MAKE IT EVEN BY DISCARDING FROM ONE SIDE ON A WINNER FROM THE OTHER.

(42) WORST FIRST

Neither side vulnerable
Dealer South

North
♠ K 8
♡ A K Q 9
♢ J 8 7 6
♣ 10 5 4

South
♠ A Q 10
♡ J 10 5
♢ 10 9 3
♣ A Q 6 2

South	West	North	East
1 ♣	Pass	1 ♡	Pass
1 NT	Pass	3 NT	All Pass

Opening lead: ♠ 2

What is your plan?

WORST FIRST (Solution)

North
♠ K 8
♡ A K Q 9
◇ J 8 7 6
♣ 10 5 4

West
♠ J 7 3 2
♡ 8 3 2
◇ A K 2
♣ K 8 7

East
♠ 9 6 5 4
♡ 7 6 4
◇ Q 5 4
♣ J 9 3

South
♠ A Q 10
♡ J 10 5
◇ 10 9 3
♣ A Q 6 2

You start life with eight sure tricks and there are two possibilities for a ninth trick—(1) the club finesse and/or the club jack dropping singleton or doubleton—: (2) a long diamond.

The opening lead tells you that spades are breaking 4-4. This means that you can let the opponents have the lead THREE times (in diamonds) and lose no more than one spade trick.

Obviously it is safer to work with diamonds than clubs. If you finesse the club and it loses you will be at the mercy of the jack of clubs dropping doubleton. Why put yourself in this predicament? Play safe.

KEY LESSON POINTERS

1. IF YOU CAN AFFORD TO GIVE UP THE LEAD, IT IS ALMOST ALWAYS RIGHT AT A NOTRUMP CONTRACT TO DEVELOP TRICKS IN SUITS WHERE YOU HAVE SURE LOSERS IN ANY CASE. IDEALLY THIS MEANS DRIVING OUT AN ACE OR AN ACE-KING IN THE SAME SUIT. IN THIS EXTREME CASE IT MEANS DRIVING OUT AN ACE-KING-QUEEN IN THE SAME SUIT. DO NOT CREATE EXTRA LOSERS FOR YOURSELF IF YOU CAN AVOID IT.
2. CHECK THE OPENING LEAD TO DETERMINE HOW THAT SUIT IS BREAKING. THE LEAD OF THE LOWEST CARD (ASSUMING FOURTH BEST LEADS) INDICATES A FOUR CARD SUIT. IF A THREE IS LED, LOOK AROUND FOR THE DEUCE. IF YOU SEE IT, YOU KNOW THE OPENING LEADER HAS LED FROM A FOUR CARD SUIT. IF YOU DON'T, THEN THE OPENING LEADER MAY WELL HAVE LED FROM A FIVE CARD SUIT.

(43) BE A SPORT

East-West vulnerable
Dealer South

North
♠ A Q 9 5
♡ J 8
◇ J 8 6 5
♣ 9 7 3

South
♠ K J
♡ A 5 4 2
◇ A K 9 2
♣ A Q 8

South	West	North	East
2 NT	Pass	3 ♣*	Pass
3 ♡	Pass	3 NT	All Pass

*Asking for a four card major

Opening lead: ◇ 3

You play low from dummy and East plays the four. What is your plan?

BE A SPORT (Solution)

North

♠ A Q 9 5
♡ J 8
◇ J 8 6 5
♣ 9 7 3

West

♠ 7 4 3
♡ 9 7 3
◇ Q 10 7 3
♣ K J 10

East

♠ 10 8 6 2
♡ K Q 10 6
◇ 4
♣ 6 5 4 2

South

♠ K J
♡ A 5 4 2
◇ A K 9 2
♣ A Q 8

Count your tricks! You have three sure spade tricks, four if either the ten drops or you can get to dummy after you unblock the KJ; one heart, three diamonds and one club for a total of eight.

If you could somehow take four spade tricks you would have no trouble at all with this hand.

Consider the diamond position. West has apparently led from Q10xx and you have three sure tricks in the suit. The point is that you have three sure tricks in the suit even if you win the first trick with the ace or king!

By doing just that you will have created a LATER entry to dummy in the form of the jack of diamonds. After you win the first diamond HIGH, cash the king-jack of spades, a second high diamond and lead a low diamond towards the jack. West wins the queen but you have the later diamond entry, not to mention nine tricks regardless of the location of the club king.

KEY LESSON POINTERS

1. WHEN A SUIT IS BLOCKED (SPADES) AND THERE IS A DEARTH OF EN-TRIES TO THE LONG HAND (THE HAND THAT IS LONGER IN THE BLOCKED SUIT) THERE ARE AT LEAST TWO POSSIBILITIES:
   (1) OVERTAKE THE SECOND SPADE AND HOPE THE KEY CARD EITHER DROPS (THE TEN IN THIS CASE) OR THAT THE SUIT SPLITS EVENLY (IF YOU HAD K J FACING AQxxx)
   (2) CREATE A SIDE ENTRY TO THE LONG HAND BY PURPOSELY WIN-NING A TRICK IN ANOTHER SUIT WITH A HIGHER CARD THAN NECESSARY.

(44) WHAT IF?

Both sides vulnerable
Dealer South

North

♠ 8 7 5
♡ 6 2
♢ A Q 6 5 2
♣ K Q 10

South

♠ 9 6 2
♡ A K J 10 4 3
♢ K J
♣ A 5

South	West	North	East
1 ♡	Pass	2 ♢	Pass
3 ♡	Pass	4 ♡	All Pass

Opening lead: ♠ K

East signals with the ten and West continues with the ace and a low spade to East's queen. At trick four East shifts to a low club. Plan the play.

WHAT IF? (Solution)

North
♠ 8 7 5
♡ 6 2
♢ A Q 6 5 2
♣ K Q 10

West
♠ A K J 4
♡ 5
♢ 9 8 4 3
♣ 9 4 3 2

East
♠ Q 10 3
♡ Q 9 8 7
♢ 10 7
♣ J 8 7 6

South
♠ 9 6 2
♡ A K J 10 4 3
♢ K J
♣ A 5

You have no losers outside of the trump suit so the problem is easy—how to play this trump suit for no losers?

In order to understand the play of the trump suit you must see the difference between the trump holding in the diagram hand as opposed to this trump suit: AKJ10x facing xxx.

Notice that in both cases you have ALL the missing honors save the queen, but in one case the suit is divided 6-2 and in the other 5-3. The difference is that in one case (when the suit is divided 5-3) you can lead a high honor and still be able to take TWO finesses if necessary because you remain with two cards in dummy. In other words, you can cater to a singleton queen in back of you as well as four to the queen in front of you.

Unfortunately, you cannot do both when you have six facing two. If you lead a high honor first you do pick up a stiff queen to your left but, alas, you will not be able to pick up four to the queen to your right. As four to the queen to your right is four times more likely than a singleton queen to your left, you should finesse immediately. Win the club return in dummy and lead a low heart to the JACK. When this holds enter dummy with a diamond to repeat the heart finesse.

KEY LESSON POINTERS

1. WITH AKJ10(x)(xx) FACING xx TAKE THE FIRST ROUND FINESSE.
2. WITH AKJ10(x) FACING xxx, CASH THE ACE AND THEN FINESSE.
3. WITH AKJxx(x) FACING xx, CASH THE ACE AND THEN FINESSE. LACKING THE TEN YOU CANNOT TAKE TWO FINESSES.

(45) SIMPLICITY

East-West vulnerable
Dealer South

North
♠ 10 3
♡ Q 10 9
♢ A J 10 9 7
♣ Q 4 3

South
♠ K 5
♡ A K 2
♢ Q 5 4 3
♣ A K 6 2

South	West	North	East
1 ♣	Pass	1 ♢	Pass
2 NT	Pass	3 NT	All Pass

Opening lead: ♠ 7

East wins with the ace and returns the nine of spades, West following with the four. Your turn.

SIMPLICITY (Solution)

North

♠ 10 3
♡ Q 10 9
♢ A J 10 9 7
♣ Q 4 3

West

♠ Q J 8 7 4 2
♡ 5 4 3
♢ 6
♣ J 9 8

East

♠ A 9 6
♡ J 8 7 6
♢ K 8 2
♣ 10 7 5

South

♠ K 5
♡ A K 2
♢ Q 5 4 3
♣ A K 6 2

You have eight top tricks, one spade, three hearts, one diamond and three clubs and need but one more trick to secure your contract.

That extra trick can either come from the diamond finesse or a possible 3-3 club division. If you could only try one you would try the finesse because that is a 50-50 proposition, whereas a 3-3 division is only 36%. But when you can try both. . . .

Play off three rounds of clubs and see if they break 3-3. If they do, you have your nine tricks and should not risk the diamond finesse. Only if clubs do not divide evenly should you attempt the diamond finesse.

KEY LESSON POINTERS

1. A SIMPLE FINESSE IS A 50-50 PROPOSITION (FOR EVERYONE ELSE, THAT IS.)
2. A 3-3 DIVISION OCCURS 36% OF THE TIME.
3. IF FORCED TO TAKE ONE PLAY OR THE OTHER, SELECT THE FINESSE. IF YOU HAVE TIME FOR BOTH, TRY FOR THE 3-3 SPLIT AND FAILING THAT, GO FOR THE FINESSE.

(46) DUCK SOUP

East-West vulnerable
Dealer North

North
♠ Q 10 9 7 6
♡ A K 7
◇ 8 4
♣ J 6 2

South
♠ A K 8 5 4
♡ 6
◇ Q 10 2
♣ Q 7 5 3

North	East	South	West
Pass	Pass	1 ♠	Pass
3 ♠	All Pass		

Opening lead: ♡ J

You win in dummy and play the ace and queen of spades, East discarding a heart on the second spade. How do you continue?

DUCK SOUP (Solution)

North

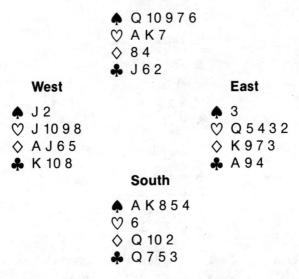

North
- ♠ Q 10 9 7 6
- ♡ A K 7
- ◇ 8 4
- ♣ J 6 2

West
- ♠ J 2
- ♡ J 10 9 8
- ◇ A J 6 5
- ♣ K 10 8

East
- ♠ 3
- ♡ Q 5 4 3 2
- ◇ K 9 7 3
- ♣ A 9 4

South
- ♠ A K 8 5 4
- ♡ 6
- ◇ Q 10 2
- ♣ Q 7 5 3

You have two diamond losers and three possible club losers, particularly if you have to break clubs. All bridge players have learned to hate the sight of an unsupported jack facing an unsupported queen. It is just not a healthy suit—unless you can force the opponents to break the suit first. On this hand you can!

Simply cash a second heart discarding a diamond, and ruff a heart. By discarding a diamond you have evened off the diamond suit between your hand and dummy—always good for a throw in.

Now exit with a diamond. The opponents can cash two diamonds but must break clubs or give you a ruff and a sluff. Either way you lose just two club tricks.

KEY LESSON POINTERS

1. THERE ARE INNUMERABLE CARD COMBINATIONS WHERE IT BENEFITS THE DECLARER TO HAVE THE SUIT LED FIRST. ONE OF THE MOST OBVIOUS IS Jxx FACING Qxx(x).
2. IN ORDER TO FORCE THE OPPONENTS TO LEAD A SUIT, YOU MUST REMOVE ALL OF THEIR SAFE EXIT CARDS FIRST. IN THIS CASE BY DRAWING TRUMPS AND REMOVING HEARTS FROM BOTH HANDS YOU HAVE REMOVED ALL OF THEIR SAFE MAJOR SUIT EXIT CARDS. BY EVENING OUT THE DIAMOND SUIT (TWO FACING TWO) YOU MAKE IT IMPOSSIBLE FOR THE OPPONENTS TO PLAY A THIRD DIAMOND WITHOUT LOSING A TRICK. NOTICE THAT IF YOU HAD DISCARDED A CLUB ON A HIGH HEART YOU WOULD NOT HAVE MADE THIS HAND AGAINST BEST DEFENSE.
3. EVENLY DIVIDED SUITS MAKE GOOD THROW-IN SUITS. AMEN.

(47) THE INEVITABLE SWITCH

Neither side vulnerable
Dealer West

North

♠ A Q 10 6
♡ 10 4 3 2
♢ 4 3 2
♣ K Q

South

♠ 3 2
♡ A K Q 9 8 7
♢ K J
♣ 5 3 2

West	North	East	South
Pass	Pass	Pass	1 ♡
Pass	3 ♡	Pass	4 ♡
All Pass			

Opening lead: ♣ 10

East wins the ace and switches to the inevitable low diamond. There you are again. Which diamond do you play, or is it just a guess?

THE INEVITABLE SWITCH (Solution)

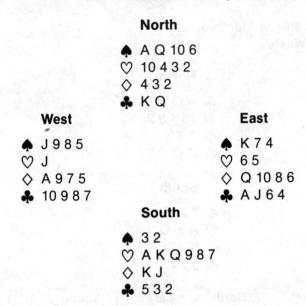

North
- ♠ A Q 10 6
- ♡ 10 4 3 2
- ◇ 4 3 2
- ♣ K Q

West
- ♠ J 9 8 5
- ♡ J
- ◇ A 9 7 5
- ♣ 10 9 8 7

East
- ♠ K 7 4
- ♡ 6 5
- ◇ Q 10 8 6
- ♣ A J 6 4

South
- ♠ 3 2
- ♡ A K Q 9 8 7
- ◇ K J
- ♣ 5 3 2

It's not a guess. Forget about diamonds for a moment and look at the whole hand. You have lost a club and you could lose a spade and two diamonds if everything goes wrong. In fact, if the AQ of diamonds are with West and the king of spades with East, you won't make the hand—but there is nothing you can do about that—. Don't worry about what you cannot help, only about what you can.

Consider the location of the king of spades for a moment. If West has that card the contract is assured regardless of what you play in diamonds. Therefore assume East has the king of spades.

Assuming East has the king of spades makes it easier to work with diamonds. If East has the king of spades and the A J of clubs (known) then he is highly unlikely to have the ace of diamonds as well. After all, he was third seat notvulnerable and might have dug up an opening bid with 12 high card points. Play the JACK of diamonds.

KEY LESSON POINTERS

1. WHEN YOU ARE IN A GOOD CONTRACT (LIKE THIS ONE) ASSUME THE WORST (KING OF SPADES WRONG) AND WORK FROM THERE.
   IF YOU ARE IN A TERRIBLE CONTRACT, (SAY FIVE HEARTS) ASSUME EVERYTHING IS RIGHT. WITH THE SAME DEFENSE ASSUME THE KING OF SPADES IS WITH WEST. UNFORTUNATELY, THAT WOULDN'T HELP YOU WITH THE DIAMOND SUIT BUT AT LEAST YOU WOULD BE THINKING LIKE A BRIDGE PLAYER. I KNOW, YOU WOULD RATHER GUESS THE DIAMOND SUIT RIGHT THAN THINK LIKE A BRIDGE PLAYER.

(48) YE OLDE 4-3

North-South vulnerable
Dealer South

North
♠ Q J 5
♡ 8 6 4
◇ J 10 9
♣ K 9 8 7

South
♠ A K 10 9
♡ 3
◇ A 4 3
♣ A Q J 10 3

South	West	North	East
1 ♣	1 ♡	2 ♣	3 ♡*
3 ♠	Pass	4 ♠	All Pass

*Preemptive

Opening lead: ♡ K

In theory, North denied four spades when he raised to two clubs. With four spades he would either make a negative double or bid the suit depending upon system. Therefore, North decided it was safe to raise a SECOND suit immediately with only three card support—a usual bridge no-no.

In any case East plays the queen of hearts at trick one, showing the jack, and West continues with the ace of hearts. Plan the play.

YE OLDE 4-3 (Solution)

North
♠ Q J 5
♡ 8 6 4
♢ J 10 9
♣ K 9 8 7

West
♠ 8 6 4 3
♡ A K 10 9 2
♢ Q 8
♣ 5 2

East
♠ 7 2
♡ Q J 7 5
♢ K 7 6 5 2
♣ 6 4

South
♠ A K 10 9
♡ 3
♢ A 4 3
♣ A Q J 10 3

If it were South's lead on the go, he could take the first ten tricks without breathing hard because he would be able to draw FOUR rounds of trumps before running the clubs.

However with the continued heart plays, (the best defense against a 4-3 trump fit with a running side suit is the forcing game) South must be careful.

If South ruffs in the long hand reducing himself to three trumps and the opposing trumps divide normally, (4-2), terminal complications usually set in.

In order to avoid ruffing in the long hand, South should discard diamonds on the second and third round of hearts leaving dummy void in hearts. If the opponents persist in hearts, the force can be taken in the SHORT hand, the dummy. Four rounds of trumps can be drawn and the club suit run for those same ten tricks.

KEY LESSON POINTERS

1. THE BEST DEFENSE AGAINST A 4-3 TRUMP FIT WITH A RUNNING SIDE SUIT, IS TO FORCE THE HAND WITH THE FOUR CARD TRUMP HOLDING TO TRUMP. THE BEST COUNTERMEASURE IS NOT TO TRUMP, BUT TO DISCARD LOSERS UNTIL THE THREE CARD TRUMP HOLDING IS VOID IN THE SUIT THE OPPONENTS ARE LEADING. ONCE THAT HAPPENS, THE SHORT HAND CAN TAKE THE SUBSEQUENT FORCE LEAVING FOUR TRUMPS IN THE LONG HAND TO DRAW A POSSIBLE FOUR ROUNDS OF TRUMPS.

2. WHEN PLAYING 4-3 TRUMP FITS WITH A SOLID SIDE SUIT, COUNT TRICKS RATHER THAN LOSERS.

(49) KNOWING YOUR CUSTOMERS

East-West vulnerable
Dealer South

North
♠ K 8 5
♡ 10 6 3
♢ K 6 4
♣ A K 10 7

South
♠ A 2
♡ A K 8 7 4 2
♢ 7 5 3 2
♣ 4

South	West	North	East
1 ♡	Pass	2 NT	Pass
3 ♡	Pass	4 ♡	All Pass

Opening lead: ♢ Q

You duck in dummy and West continues with the ten of diamonds which you duck again. No luck—the ten holds. West plays a third diamond to East's ace. At trick four East shifts to the three of spades.

You win in dummy and lead the TEN of hearts. East covers with the jack and West's queen falls under your ace.

How do you continue against (1) weak opponents, (2) strong opponents?

KNOWING YOUR CUSTOMERS (Solution)

North
♠ K 8 5
♡ 10 6 3
♢ K 6 4
♣ A K 10 7

West
♠ J 9 7 4
♡ Q 9
♢ Q J 10
♣ Q 9 3 2

East
♠ Q 10 6 3
♡ J 5
♢ A 9 8
♣ J 8 6 5

South
♠ A 2
♡ A K 8 7 4 2
♢ 7 5 3 2
♣ 4

Against weak opponents you should enter dummy with a club and lead a heart to the eight.

A weak West player would never be clever enough to drop the queen of hearts holding queen-nine doubleton—even though they are both equals at this point.

Against strong opponents cash a second high heart. There are two reasons for this.

(1) A strong East player would not cover the ten of hearts holding J 9 5. Why should he? If partner has a heart honor the hand is always defeated by playing low. If partner does not have a heart honor, covering won't help.

(2) A strong West player would be very apt to drop the queen of hearts from queen-nine doubleton as they are both equals at this stage.

Why lead the ten of hearts in the first place?

(1) If East has all four hearts he is apt to cover the ten even though you were not planning to finesse. If he does cover, you go down one instead of two.

(2) Weak players frequently go wrong in covering situations. Many an East player would cover the ten holding J 9 5, crashing partner's queen.

KEY LESSON POINTERS

1. IF IT CANNOT COST YOU TO LEAD EITHER AN HONOR FROM YOUR HAND TOWARD DUMMY, OR AN HONOR FROM DUMMY TOWARD YOUR HAND, EVEN THOUGH YOU HAVE NO INTENTION OF FINESSING, BY ALL MEANS DO SO. THOUSANDS OF TRICKS ARE LOST ANNUALLY BY DEFENDERS WHO COVER INDISCRIMINATELY.

(50) FIGHTING A PREEMPT

North-South vulnerable
Dealer West

North

♠ A 8 6 5
♡ Q 6
♢ A J 10 9
♣ A K 3

South

♠ K Q 7 3 2
♡ 7 3
♢ K 4 3 2
♣ Q 2

West	North	East	South
4 ♡	Dbl.	Pass	4 ♠
All Pass			

Opening lead: ♡ K

West continues with the ace of hearts, East playing high-low. At trick three West shifts to the nine of clubs which you win with the queen. You play three high spades, West discarding three hearts. West follows to the second club, but discards yet another heart on the third round of clubs while you discard the deuce of diamonds. How do you play the diamonds?

FIGHTING A PREEMPT (Solution)

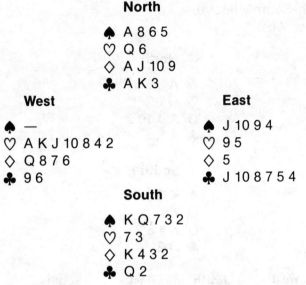

North
- ♠ A 8 6 5
- ♡ Q 6
- ◇ A J 10 9
- ♣ A K 3

West
- ♠ —
- ♡ A K J 10 8 4 2
- ◇ Q 8 7 6
- ♣ 9 6

East
- ♠ J 10 9 4
- ♡ 9 5
- ◇ 5
- ♣ J 10 8 7 5 4

South
- ♠ K Q 7 3 2
- ♡ 7 3
- ◇ K 4 3 2
- ♣ Q 2

Are you counting? West should have seven hearts, judging from his four level preempt and East's high-low. West is known to have two clubs and to be void in spades. His hand counts out beautifully. It must be 0-7-4-2.

Knowing that West has four diamonds and East, perforce, a singleton makes life a joy. All you need do is lead a diamond to the king and finesse the ten on the way back. You lose two hearts and a spade . . . period.

KEY LESSON POINTERS

1. WHEN ONE PLAYER TURNS UP WITH A KNOWN LONG SUIT, KEEP COUNT OF HIS HAND ONLY.
2. WHEN MISSING A QUEEN THAT CAN BE FINESSED EITHER WAY, PLAY THE OTHER SUITS FIRST, IF POSSIBLE, TRYING FOR A COUNT.
3. IN THE MISSING QUEEN SUIT, PLAY THE HAND THAT WAS DEALT THE LONGER HOLDING IN THE SUIT FOR THE QUEEN. THERE ARE ONLY TWO EXCEPTIONS TO THIS RULE: (AREN'T YOU GLAD TO HEAR THAT?)
   A. IF THE PLAYER WITH THE ORIGINAL LENGTH HAS DISCARDED DOWN TO A DOUBLETON AND THE OTHER PLAYER IS ALSO KNOWN TO HOLD A DOUBLETON, PLAY FOR THE DROP. (THIS DOESN'T HAPPEN OFTEN AGAINST GOOD PLAYERS.)
   B. IF THE PLAYER WITH THE SHORTNESS MUST HAVE THE QUEEN TO JUSTIFY HIS BIDDING, GO AGAINST THE ODDS AND PLAY THE SHORT HAND FOR THE QUEEN. IN ALL OTHER CASES, PLAY THE LONG HAND FOR THE QUEEN.

(51) PSYCHOLOGY

East-West vulnerable
Dealer West

North

♠ Q J 4 3
♡ J 4
♢ A Q 7 5 3
♣ 3 2

South

♠ K 10 2
♡ A 7 6 3
♢ J 10
♣ A K Q 5

West	North	East	South
1 ♡	Pass	Pass	1 NT
Pass	2 ♡*	Pass	2 NT
Pass	3 NT	All Pass	

*Stayman, asking for a four card major.

Opening lead: ♡ K

You duck the opening lead as well as the continuation of the queen of hearts. At trick three West continues with the ten of hearts.

On the third heart, East discards a small spade. What do you discard from dummy, and what is your plan?

PSYCHOLOGY (Solution)

North

♠ Q J 4 3
♡ J 4
♢ A Q 7 5 3
♣ 3 2

West

♠ A 8
♡ K Q 10 9 2
♢ K 6 2
♣ J 10 7

East

♠ 9 7 6 5
♡ 8 5
♢ 9 8 4
♣ 9 8 6 4

South

♠ K 10 2
♡ A 7 6 3
♢ J 10
♣ A K Q 5

It is quite clear that West has all the missing high cards to justify the opening bid. Since West started with five hearts you cannot afford to knock out the ace of spades as you will lose four hearts plus a spade.

The better chance is to try for five diamond tricks. However this is not so easy as the suit is blocked. Assume you lead the jack and West covers. Now what? You can win the ace, and cross back to the ten but you will have to lead a spade to get back over to the good diamonds. No, that won't work.

What if you discard a spade from dummy and lead the TEN of diamonds. True, West can cover and block the suit. But human nature being what it is, West is more likely to duck the ten than the jack. If West ducks the ten, lead the jack, overtaking with the queen (if West ducks again) and score five diamonds, three clubs and a heart.

KEY LESSON POINTERS

1. WHEN THE DUMMY COMES DOWN, ADD YOUR HIGH CARD POINTS TO DUMMY'S HIGH CARD POINTS. YOU HAVE 17 AND DUMMY HAS 10 FOR A GRAND TOTAL OF 27. THIS LEAVES THE OPPONENTS WITH 13 AND WEST HAS OPENED THE BIDDING. IT DOESN'T TAKE A SUPER BRAIN TO FIGURE OUT THAT WEST HAS ALL OF THE MISSING HIGH CARDS, SAVE PERHAPS A JACK. GOOD HABIT TO GET INTO—COUNTING UP THE TOTAL POINTS BETWEEN YOUR HAND AND DUMMY.

2. WHEN PLAYING A SUIT THAT HAS EQUAL HONORS: IF YOU WANT THE OPPONENTS TO COVER, PLAY THE HIGHER OR THE HIGHEST EQUAL, IF YOU WANT THE OPPONENTS TO DUCK, PLAY THE LOWER OR THE LOWEST EQUAL. IT WORKS!

(52) ERROR!

East-West vulnerable
Dealer South

North
♠ J 5 2
♡ J 10 9
◇ A 9 4 2
♣ Q 8 7

South
♠ 9 6 3
♡ A K Q 7 5
◇ 3
♣ A K 3 2

South	West	North	East
1 ♡	Pass	1 NT	Pass
2 ♣	Pass	2 ♡	Pass
3 ♡	Pass	4 ♡	All Pass

Opening lead: ♠ K

West continues with the queen and a spade to East's ace. East shifts to the king of diamonds at trick four. Plan the play.

ERROR! (Solution)

North

♠ J 5 2
♡ J 10 9
♢ A 9 4 2
♣ Q 8 7

West

♠ K Q 7
♡ 6 4 2
♢ 10 8 7 6 5
♣ J 9

East

♠ A 10 8 4
♡ 8 3
♢ K Q J
♣ 10 6 5 4

South

♠ 9 6 3
♡ A K Q 7 5
♢ 3
♣ A K 3 2

Your only loser is your fourth club. Given that you cannot discard it on a side suit winner from dummy, there are still three other ways to avoid losing that card. (1) The suit breaks 3-3. (2) Draw two rounds of trumps and then play three rounds of clubs. If clubs are 4-2 and the player with the remaining trump(s) has the LONG clubs, you can RUFF the fourth club in dummy. (3) Discard it on a trump!

In order to do (3) you must ruff three cards in your own hand leaving dummy with one more trump than you. On that extra trump you can discard your club.

Win the ace of diamonds and ruff a diamond high. Cross to the nine of hearts and ruff a second diamond high. You now have two trumps in each hand. Cross to dummy with the ten of trumps and ruff the last diamond with your last trump. Enter dummy with the queen of clubs and discard your fourth club on dummy's jack of hearts. A dummy reversal.

KEY LESSON POINTERS

1. 5-3 TRUMP FITS WITH ONE OR TWO HIGH TRUMP HONORS IN THE SHORT HAND LEND THEMSELVES TO DUMMY REVERSALS WHEN THERE IS A SHORT SUIT IN THE LONG HAND.
2. BY RUFFING THREE TIMES IN THE LONG HAND, THE DUMMY HAND WINDS UP WITH ONE EXTRA TRUMP. ON THAT EXTRA TRUMP A LOSER CAN BE DISCARDED. RUFFING TWICE IN THE LONG HAND DOES NOT HELP.
3. THE ERROR (SEE TITLE) WAS EAST'S RETURN AT TRICK FOUR. A TRUMP DOES YOU IN, REMOVING A DUMMY ENTRY PREMATURELY.

(53) THEY'RE WAITING

Both sides vulnerable
Dealer South

North

♠ A J 8
♡ 10 7 3 2
♢ Q 10 8 4
♣ 9 6

South

♠ K 7 5 2
♡ Q J 4
♢ A K 3
♣ A 10 2

South	West	North	East
1 NT*	All Pass		

*15–17

Opening lead: ♣ 4

East plays the queen which you allow to hold. East continues with the king which you duck, West playing the three. East continues with a third club which you must win, perforce.

What do you discard from dummy, and what is your plan?

THEY'RE WAITING (Solution)

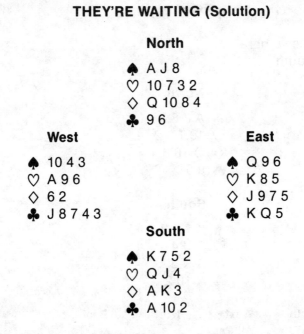

North
- ♠ A J 8
- ♡ 10 7 3 2
- ◇ Q 10 8 4
- ♣ 9 6

West
- ♠ 10 4 3
- ♡ A 9 6
- ◇ 6 2
- ♣ J 8 7 4 3

East
- ♠ Q 9 6
- ♡ K 8 5
- ◇ J 9 7 5
- ♣ K Q 5

South
- ♠ K 7 5 2
- ♡ Q J 4
- ◇ A K 3
- ♣ A 10 2

Not only must you count YOUR tricks at a notrump contract, you must also count THEIRS!

You have six sure tricks; two spades, three diamonds and a club with a possibility of at least one extra trick in each suit except clubs.

But what do they have? They have two clubs already as well as two more waiting to be taken. They also own the two top hearts for a total of six tricks.

This whole hand is a battle for the seventh trick. Don't give it to them on a silver platter by either finessing the spade or trying to drop the jack of diamonds. Play the suit in which they have the sure trick(s), HEARTS.

Discard a spade from dummy and lead a heart honor. If West wins and cashes two clubs you can throw two spades from your hand and a couple of hearts from dummy.

Assuming a spade switch, win the ace and lead the ten of hearts driving out the king and establishing your jack of hearts for the seventh trick.

KEY LESSON POINTERS

1. COUNT YOUR TRICKS AS WELL AS THEIRS IN A NOTRUMP CONTRACT.
2. TRY TO DEVELOP TRICKS IN SUITS IN WHICH THEY ALREADY HAVE THE HIGH CARDS. THOSE ARE LOSERS IN ANY CASE. DON'T INCREASE THE TOTAL IF YOU CAN HELP IT.
3. WATCH THE LEAD AND THE RETURN TO SEE HOW THE SUIT LED IS BREAKING. IT IS IMPORTANT TO KNOW HOW MANY TRICKS THEY CAN TAKE IN THAT SUIT ONCE THEY REGAIN THE LEAD.

(54) THREATS LAST

Both sides vulnerable
Dealer South

North

♠ K Q 6
♡ Q J 6
♢ Q 6 3
♣ A K 4 2

South

♠ A J 3
♡ A K 10
♢ A K 4 2
♣ Q 6 5

South	West	North	East
2 NT	Pass	7 NT	All Pass

Opening lead: ♠ 10

What is your plan?

THREATS LAST (Solution)

North

♠ K Q 6
♡ Q J 6
♢ Q 6 3
♣ A K 4 2

West	East
♠ 10 9 8 7	♠ 5 4 2
♡ 8 5 4 3 2	♡ 9 7
♢ 7 5	♢ J 10 9 8
♣ 7 3	♣ J 10 9 8

South

♠ A J 3
♡ A K 10
♢ A K 4 2
♣ Q 6 5

You have three sure tricks in each suit for a grand total of twelve. Besides, you have a chance of an extra trick if either minor suit breaks 3-3. What to do?

In order to understand the play of this hand you must be familiar with these two terms: (1) threat suit (2) non-threat suit.

Take a look at your major suits. You have three tricks in each suit and can never take more even if the opponents discard all of their spades and hearts. Any suit which cannot take extra tricks regardless of the number of cards discarded by the opponents is called a NON-THREAT SUIT.

Now look at your minor suits. You can conceivably take an extra trick in either minor suit if, for example, an opponent with either four clubs or four diamonds discards as few as one card in the suit. Suits which can conceivably provide extra tricks are called THREAT SUITS.

When playing a contract in which you have all the tricks but one, play NON-THREAT SUITS FIRST. Notice that East must make one discard on the third heart. Whichever minor suit East discards gives you an extra trick in that suit. Don't tell anybody, but you have just executed a simple squeeze play!

KEY LESSON POINTERS

1. WHEN PLAYING A NOTRUMP CONTRACT, IF YOU HAVE ALL THE TRICKS BUT ONE, PLAY WINNERS IN YOUR NON-THREAT SUIT(S) BEFORE WINNERS IN YOUR THREAT SUIT(S).
2. WHEN PLAYING A SUIT CONTRACT WITH ALL THE TRICKS BUT ONE, PLAY ALL THE WINNERS IN YOUR NON-THREAT SUIT(S) (INCLUDING YOUR LAST TRUMP) BEFORE YOUR THREAT SUITS.

(55) BIG ASSUMPTIONS

East-West vulnerable
Dealer East

North
♠ A J 4
♡ J 3 2
♢ A K J
♣ 10 8 7 5

South
♠ K 10 2
♡ K 9 6
♢ Q 6 5
♣ Q J 9 2

East	South	West	North
Pass	Pass	Pass	1 ♣
Pass	2 NT	Pass	3 NT
All Pass			

Opening lead: ♢ 10

You win the king in dummy, East plays the deuce. At trick two you lead a club to the queen which wins. You play a second club which East wins with the king, West following high-low.

East returns a second diamond which you win in dummy. You play a third club to East's ace, West discarding the seven of hearts. East stubbornly plays a third diamond, all following. West has played the seven and eight of diamonds on subsequent diamond plays and can be assumed to hold the established nine of diamonds.

You lead a fourth round of clubs ending in dummy and West discards a lower heart and East a low spade. How do you continue?

BIG ASSUMPTIONS (Solution)

North

♠ A J 4
♡ J 3 2
◇ A K J
♣ 10 8 7 5

West

♠ Q 9 8
♡ Q 7 5 4
◇ 10 9 8 7
♣ 4 3

East

♠ 7 6 5 3
♡ A 10 8
◇ 4 3 2
♣ A K 6

South

♠ K 10 2
♡ K 9 6
◇ Q 6 5
♣ Q J 9 2

You have two sure clubs, three sure diamonds and two sure spades for a grand total of seven tricks. Even if you guess spades correctly you only have eight tricks. Therefore you must find the ace of hearts in the East hand to make your contract.

Lead a heart to the king, and assuming it holds, play WEST for the queen of spades. Why? Because East has already turned up with the A K of clubs and the ace of hearts. With the queen of spades he would have opened the bidding. He is a passed hand—remember?

If it turns out that West has the ace of hearts, forget it. You were never going to make this hand anyway.

KEY LESSON POINTERS

1. WHEN YOU NEED A SPECIFIC HIGH CARD IN A CERTAIN PLACE TO EVEN HAVE A CHANCE TO MAKE YOUR CONTRACT, ASSUME IT IS THERE. IF YOU CAN FIND OUT, FINE, IF YOU CAN'T, PLAY ON THE ASSUMPTION IT IS WHERE YOU WANT IT TO BE. THAT MAY HELP YOU LOCATE OTHER HONOR CARDS.
2. DON'T BE AFRAID TO GO DOWN A COUPLE OF EXTRA TRICKS TO RISK MAKING YOUR CONTRACT. DON'T PLAY LIKE A COWARD. IT IS NOT BECOMING. PARTNERS WILL RESPECT YOU MORE WHEN YOU TRY TO MAKE UNDOUBLED CONTRACTS RATHER THAN SETTLING FOR A SMALL MINUS SCORE.

(56) CHIN UP

East-West vulnerable
Dealer South

North
- ♠ 10 6
- ♡ A 10 9 8
- ♢ 10 8 4
- ♣ K J 10 9

South
- ♠ Q J 8
- ♡ K Q J
- ♢ A K 9 7 3
- ♣ Q 4

South	West	North	East
1 ♢	1 ♠	Dbl.*	Pass
2 NT	Pass	3 NT	All Pass

*Negative Double—promising at least four hearts plus
scattered values.

Opening lead: ♠ 7

Which spade do you play from dummy, and what is your plan?

CHIN UP (Solution)

North

♠ 10 6
♡ A 10 9 8
◇ 10 8 4
♣ K J 10 9

West

♠ A K 9 7 3 2
♡ 3 2
◇ 2
♣ A 8 7 6

East

♠ 5 4
♡ 7 6 5 4
◇ Q J 6 5
♣ 5 3 2

South

♠ Q J 8
♡ K Q J
◇ A K 9 7 3
♣ Q 4

In case you don't know it, you are in big trouble! West has probably led from a five or six card spade suit and unless you wish to see spades raining down upon you, you cannot afford to drive out the club ace.

Back to basics. How many sure tricks are there? You have one spade, four hearts, and two diamonds for a grand total of seven. Under more normal circumstances you would drive out the ace of clubs—but on this hand you cannot afford to give up the lead so you must concentrate on DIAMONDS.

The best play in diamonds to avoid a loser is to take a double finesse through East. In other words, play East for both missing honors.

Win the ten of spades in dummy (the rule of eleven tells you that East has no card higher than the seven) and run the ten of diamonds if it is not covered. If the ten holds, play a second diamond. Assuming East splits, win, cash four hearts and repeat the diamond finesse to make an overtrick. You are some player. Did you know that?

KEY LESSON POINTERS

1. PLAN YOUR PLAY BEFORE PLAYING TO THE FIRST TRICK. FOR EXAMPLE, IF YOU PLAY LOW FROM DUMMY AT TRICK ONE YOU CAN NO LONGER MAKE THIS HAND! (NOT ENOUGH ENTRIES TO FINESSE DIAMONDS TWICE.)
2. DON'T BE AFRAID TO MAKE A "BIG" PLAY (DOUBLE DIAMOND FINESSE) IF IT IS YOUR ONLY REASONABLE CHANCE.

3. THE RULE OF ELEVEN WORKS LIKE THIS: SUBTRACT THE SIZE OF THE SPOT CARD LED FROM THE NUMBER ELEVEN. THAT TELLS YOU THE NUMBER OF CARDS ABOVE THAT SPOT CARD IN THE REMAINING THREE HANDS. TAKE THIS HAND, FOR EXAMPLE. SEVEN FROM ELEVEN IS FOUR. THERE ARE FOUR CARDS HIGHER THAN THE SEVEN IN THE REMAINING THREE HANDS. DUMMY HAS ONE, YOU HAVE THREE SO EAST HAS NONE. THIS RULE ONLY WORKS WHEN A FOURTH BEST CARD IS LED. KEEP IN MIND YOU ALWAYS KNOW THAT THE OPENING LEADER HAS THREE CARDS HIGHER THAN THE ONE HE HAS LED, THE "RULE" LETS YOU KNOW HOW MANY CARDS HIGHER THE OPENING LEADER'S PARTNER HAS. THIRD HAND CAN ALSO USE THE "RULE" TO FIGURE OUT HOW MANY CARDS ABOVE THE ONE PARTNER HAS LED ARE IN THE DECLARER'S HAND.

(57) FOILED—ALMOST

Both sides vulnerable
Dealer South

North
♠ A J 10 2
♡ 9 7
♢ K 2
♣ A Q J 10 4

South
♠ K Q 9 8 7 3
♡ A J
♢ A 5 3
♣ 7 2

South	West	North	East
1 ♠	Pass	3 ♣	Pass
3 ♠	Pass	4 ♠	Pass
4 NT	Pass	5 ♡	Dbl.
5 NT	Pass	6 ♢	Pass
6 ♠	All Pass		

Opening lead: ♡ 3

East plays the queen. Plan the play.

FOILED—ALMOST (Solution)

North

♠ A J 10 2
♡ 9 7
♢ K 2
♣ A Q J 10 4

West

♠ 6
♡ 8 6 5 3 2
♢ Q J 10 4
♣ 6 5 3

East

♠ 5 4
♡ K Q 10 4
♢ 9 8 7 6
♣ K 9 8

South

♠ K Q 9 8 7 3
♡ A J
♢ A 5 3
♣ 7 2

The heart lead has complicated matters. Notice that East was alert enough to double the five heart Blackwood response to get the lead he wanted. Without the double, West would certainly have led the queen of diamonds and the slam would have been easy. Even if the club finesse loses there is no problem with a diamond lead as the heart ace is still securely in place.

With the heart lead a throw-in must be attempted. Draw trumps, strip the diamonds by ruffing one in dummy, and exit with a heart, the equal length suit.

Assuming East wins the trick he must either lead a red card allowing you to discard a club from your hand while ruffing in dummy or lead a club smack into JAWS.

Incidentally, when you lead a heart from DUMMY, (after stripping the diamonds) an expert East should play low hoping his partner has the jack of hearts. Notice that East breaks even by ducking the heart when you have the jack, (he gets a club trick) but defeats the slam when partner has that card.

KEY LESSON POINTERS

1. DEFENSIVELY, BE ON THE ALERT TO DOUBLE BLACKWOOD RESPONSES TO GET THE LEAD YOU WANT.
2. OFFENSIVELY, DO NOT FORGET TO USE YOUR EQUAL LENGTH SUIT (HEARTS IN THIS CASE) AS YOUR THROW-IN SUIT TO AVOID POSSIBLE FINESSES.

(58) INFERENCE

East-West vulnerable
Dealer South

North

♠ 6 4 3
♡ 3 2
◇ J 10 6 5
♣ K 10 7 5

South

♠ A K 5
♡ Q J 9 8
◇ K Q 4
♣ A Q 3

South	West	North	East
2 NT	Pass	3 NT	All Pass

Opening lead: ♠ 2

East plays the jack which you win with the king. You continue with the king, queen, and finally a small diamond to the ten. East wins the third diamond, West follows to the first diamond and discards two hearts on the subsequent diamonds.

East continues with the nine of spades which you duck but win the third spade, all following. How do you play the clubs, and why?

INFERENCE (Solution)

North

- ♠ 6 4 3
- ♡ 3 2
- ◇ J 10 6 5
- ♣ K 10 7 5

West

- ♠ Q 10 8 2
- ♡ A 6 5 4
- ◇ 3
- ♣ J 8 6 2

East

- ♠ J 9 7
- ♡ K 10 7
- ◇ A 9 8 7 2
- ♣ 9 4

South

- ♠ A K 5
- ♡ Q J 9 8
- ◇ K Q 4
- ♣ A Q 3

You should play West for four clubs and cash your ace-queen of clubs and lead low to the ten. Why?

First of all, you need FOUR club tricks to make your contract, so your play in the suit is vital. You have five tricks outside of clubs, three diamonds and two spades.

You know that West started with four spades and one diamond. That leaves him eight other cards. If those cards were divided 5-3, there is a good chance the opening lead would have been from a five card rather than a four card suit. Therefore, you should assume that West's original distribution was 4-4-1-4 and play the clubs accordingly.

KEY LESSON POINTERS

1. WHEN A PLAYER LEADS FROM A KNOWN FOUR CARD SUIT VS. A NOTRUMP CONTRACT AND THEN TURNS UP WITH A SINGLETON IN ANOTHER SUIT, THE ASSUMPTION IS THAT HIS ORIGINAL DISTRIBUTION WAS 4-4-4-1. THIS ASSUMPTION PRESUMES THAT NEITHER YOU NOR YOUR PARTNER HAVE BID A SUIT. IF YOU HAVE, IT IS POSSIBLE THAT THE OPENING LEADER HAS FIVE CARDS IN A BID SUIT AND ELECTED TO LEAD FROM A SHORTER UNBID SUIT INSTEAD.

(59) TWO LONG SUITS AND TWO SHORT SUITS

East-West vulnerable
Dealer South

North

♠ A 5 4 2
♡ A 10 9 5 4 3
♢ 2
♣ K 4

South

♠ K Q J 6
♡ 6
♢ A K 8 7 4 3
♣ 9 5

South	West	North	East
1 ♢	Pass	1 ♡	Pass
1 ♠	Pass	4 ♠	All Pass

Opening lead: ♣ Q

You cover and, as expected, East wins. East returns the three of clubs to West's ten. At trick three West shifts to the deuce of hearts. Plan the play.

TWO LONG SUITS AND TWO SHORT SUITS (Solution)

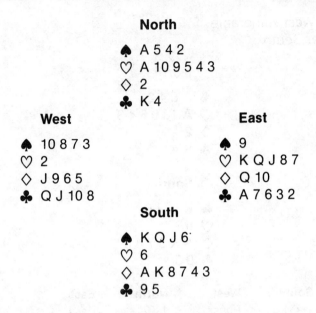

North
- ♠ A 5 4 2
- ♡ A 10 9 5 4 3
- ◇ 2
- ♣ K 4

West
- ♠ 10 8 7 3
- ♡ 2
- ◇ J 9 6 5
- ♣ Q J 10 8

East
- ♠ 9
- ♡ K Q J 8 7
- ◇ Q 10
- ♣ A 7 6 3 2

South
- ♠ K Q J 6
- ♡ 6
- ◇ A K 8 7 4 3
- ♣ 9 5

The play of hands that have both long and short suits on both sides as well as a 4-4 trump fit are dependent upon the strength of the side suits as well as the strength of the trump suit.

With high trumps on both sides think crossruff. When one hand (South) has a trump holding a great deal stronger than his partner, it is usually right to ruff in the WEAKER hand, retaining the stronger trumps for pulling purposes.

Win the ace of hearts and play ace and ruff a diamond low. Back to the king of spades and ruff a second diamond with the ace of spades. The diamonds are now good. Reenter the South hand with a trump. If both opponents follow, pull the last trump and claim.

If someone shows out, play a third high trump and run the good diamonds. The opponents can take no more than one trump trick. You have made the hand in spite of bad breaks in all of the key suits.

KEY LESSON POINTERS

1. WHEN PLAYING A 4-4 TRUMP FIT WITH LONG SUITS ON BOTH SIDES CONSIDER A CROSSRUFF IF YOU HAVE MOST OF THE HIGH TRUMPS BETWEEN THE TWO HANDS.
2. LACKING HIGH TRUMPS ON BOTH SIDES, TRY TO SET UP THE LONG SUIT IN THE HAND WITH THE STRONGER TRUMP HOLDING. THIS MEANS RUFFING IN THE HAND WITH THE WEAKER TRUMP HOLDING TO BE ABLE TO DRAW TRUMPS WITH THE HIGH TRUMPS. AVOID RUFFING IN BOTH HANDS. YOU COULD LOSE CONTROL.

(60) YES OR NO?

East-West vulnerable
Dealer South

North
- ♠ 8 4
- ♡ K 3 2
- ◇ A 10 8 3 2
- ♣ A J 2

South
- ♠ A J 6
- ♡ A J 5
- ◇ Q J 9
- ♣ K 5 4 3

South	West	North	East
1 NT	Pass	3 NT	All Pass

Opening lead: ♠ 3

East produces the king. Do you take the trick? What is your plan?

YES OR NO? (Solution)

North

♠ 8 4
♡ K 3 2
◇ A 10 8 3 2
♣ A J 2

West

♠ Q 10 7 3 2
♡ 9 8 4
◇ 7 4
♣ 9 8 7

East

♠ K 9 5
♡ Q 10 7 6
◇ K 6 5
♣ Q 10 6

South

♠ A J 6
♡ A J 5
◇ Q J 9
♣ K 5 4 3

Outside of diamonds, your best suit, you have five sure tricks, one spade, two hearts and two clubs. Clearly, you are going to have to work with diamonds.

The diamond finesse, perforce, goes into the EAST hand. If you win the first spade and the diamond finesse loses, your jack of spades will be vulnerable to an attack from East.

Obviously, it is in your best interest to duck the opening lead and win the THIRD spade. Now, if the diamond finesse loses either East has no more spades, or if he does, the suit has divided 4-4 in which case you lose three spades and a diamond.

KEY LESSON POINTERS

1. WHEN HOLDING AN AJx STOPPER OPPOSITE SMALL CARDS, WINNING OR DUCKING THE FIRST TRICK DEPENDS UPON WHICH OPPONENT IS MORE APT TO GET THE LEAD NEXT. IF IT IS YOUR RIGHT HAND OPPONENT, MAKE A HOLDUP PLAY. YOUR JACK IS WORTHLESS IN THIS CASE. IF IT IS YOUR LEFT HAND OPPONENT, WIN THE FIRST TRICK AS YOUR JACK WILL BE A FULL STOPPER AGAINST ANY FURTHER ASSAULT ON THE SUIT FROM THE LEFT.

(61) MATURITY

North-South vulnerable
Dealer South

North
♠ A 10 9 6
♡ K 9 8 7
◇ A 9
♣ 5 4 2

South
♠ K J 8 7
♡ A Q 10
◇ 3 2
♣ A 9 8 6

South	West	North	East
1 ♣	Pass	1 ♡	Pass
1 ♠	Pass	3 ♠	Pass
4 ♠	All Pass		

Opening lead: ◇ Q

Plan the play.

MATURITY (Solution)

North

♠ A 10 9 6
♡ K 9 8 7
♢ A 9
♣ 5 4 2

West

♠ 3 2
♡ J 4 2
♢ Q J 10 6
♣ K J 7 3

East

♠ Q 5 4
♡ 7 6 5
♢ K 8 7 5 4
♣ Q 10

South

♠ K J 8 7
♡ A Q 10
♢ 3 2
♣ A 9 8 6

You have a possible spade loser, a diamond loser and two clubs losers. On the plus side you have a possible extra winner in the form of a fourth heart.

You could go all out and take the spade finesse one way or the other. If you find that elusive trump lady you make the contract. If you don't, oh well.

But there is another play, a play that combines chances (the magic word) in hearts and spades. Play the ace-king of spades, if the queen drops, fine, draw the last trump and try to discard a diamond on the fourth heart. If you can, you make five, if not, four.

However, if the queen does not drop, you can always fall back on the heart suit. If hearts break 3-3 or the jack is doubleton and the player with the queen of spades has four small hearts you still make your contract. You get rid of the diamond before the queen of spades can trump a heart and cash a diamond.

KEY LESSON POINTERS

1. THE BEST PLAY IN A SUIT THAT HAS EIGHT CARDS MISSING THE QUEEN IS TO TAKE A FINESSE RATHER THAN PLAY FOR A DROP.
2. GIVEN AN EIGHT CARD TRUMP SUIT MISSING THE QUEEN, ALONG WITH A SEVEN CARD SIDE SUIT HEADED BY THE ACE-KING-QUEEN, PLUS A QUICK LOSER IN A THIRD SUIT, THE BEST PLAY IS TO CASH THE ACE-KING OF THE TRUMP SUIT AND IF THE QUEEN HAS NOT FALLEN, TEST THE SEVEN CARD SUIT FOR A 3-3 DIVISION. THIS IS BETTER THAN A SIMPLE FINESSE IN THE TRUMP SUIT.

(62) EASY DOES IT

Neither side vulnerable
Dealer South

North
♠ 4 3
♡ A K Q 6 5
◇ 8 7 6
♣ 7 4 2

South
♠ A K Q J 10
♡ 3 2
◇ A K 9
♣ A J 6

South	West	North	East
2 ♣*	Pass	2 ♡	Pass
2 ♠	Pass	3 ♡	Pass
3 NT	Pass	5 NT**	Pass
6 ♠	All Pass		

*Strong and artificial
**Pick the best slam

Opening lead: ◇ Q—East plays the deuce

Plan the play.

EASY DOES IT (Solution)

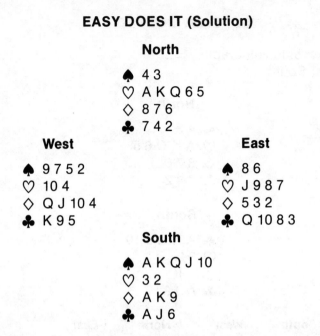

North

♠ 4 3
♡ A K Q 6 5
◇ 8 7 6
♣ 7 4 2

West

♠ 9 7 5 2
♡ 10 4
◇ Q J 10 4
♣ K 9 5

East

♠ 8 6
♡ J 9 8 7
◇ 5 3 2
♣ Q 10 8 3

South

♠ A K Q J 10
♡ 3 2
◇ A K 9
♣ A J 6

There is a diamond loser and two probable club losers. The bright side is that you have an extra winner in hearts and perhaps more depending upon the adverse division of that suit.

Now count tricks. You have five spades, three hearts, two diamonds and one club for a grand total of eleven. You need one more trick.

Consider the heart suit. If you need five tricks—the suit must divide 3-3 (36%). However, you only need FOUR tricks. Do you see it?

Win the opening lead with the ACE, draw trumps, discarding minor suits, and DUCK a heart. That's right! Let them have a heart trick. Win the minor suit return and if hearts break no worse than 4-2, you make your slam scoring five spades, FOUR hearts, two diamonds, and a club.

KEY LESSON POINTERS

1. MANY HANDS PLAYED AT A TRUMP CONTRACT BECOME NOTRUMP HANDS ONCE TRUMPS ARE REMOVED. THIS IS ONE OF THEM. FOR THAT REASON IT PAYS NOT ONLY TO COUNT LOSERS BUT TRICKS AS WELL. IF IT TURNS INTO A NOTRUMP HAND USE THE TRICK COUNT. IT MAKES LIFE EASIER.
2. WHEN WINNING A TRICK WITH ONE OF TWO EQUAL CARDS, DECLARER USUALLY DOES BEST TO WIN WITH THE HIGHER EQUAL. WIN THE OPENING LEAD WITH THE ACE OF DIAMONDS, NOT THE KING.
3. WHEN DEALING WITH A LONG SUIT IN DUMMY THAT HAS NO ENTRY OUTSIDE THE SUIT ITSELF, DETERMINE HOW MANY TRICKS YOU NEED FROM THE SUIT. IF YOU CAN AFFORD TO DUCK A ROUND OF THE SUIT TO INSURE AGAINST A BAD BREAK, BY ALL MEANS DO SO.

(63) USE EVERYTHING

East-West vulnerable
Dealer South

North
♠ 8 6 4
♡ J 5
◇ Q J 6 5
♣ A 8 3 2

South
♠ Q 9 3
♡ A K Q 10 9 8
◇ A
♣ K 7 4

South	West	North	East
1 ♡	Pass	1 NT	Pass
4 ♡	All Pass		

Opening lead: ♣ Q

East follows with the six. Plan the play.

USE EVERYTHING (Solution)

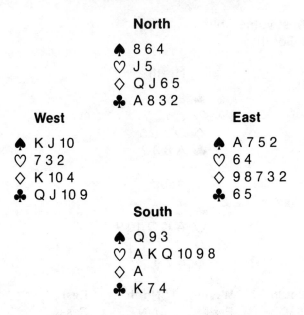

North

♠ 8 6 4
♡ J 5
♢ Q J 6 5
♣ A 8 3 2

West

♠ K J 10
♡ 7 3 2
♢ K 10 4
♣ Q J 10 9

East

♠ A 7 5 2
♡ 6 4
♢ 9 8 7 3 2
♣ 6 5

South

♠ Q 9 3
♡ A K Q 10 9 8
♢ A
♣ K 7 4

You have three spade losers, unless East has both the ace and king, plus a club loser. Do not despair. You have a hidden treasure in the diamond suit.

Win the KING of clubs, cash your red aces, enter dummy with a trump and run the queen of diamonds, discarding a SPADE if the queen is not covered.

Assuming the queen loses, the opponents can cash but TWO spade tricks. The jack of diamonds becomes the parking place for the club loser.

You have exchanged a club and a spade loser for a diamond loser. What a bargain!

KEY LESSON POINTERS

1. WHEN HOLDING TWO OR MORE EQUAL HIGH CARDS FACING A VOID AND THE OPPONENTS HAVE BUT ONE HIGHER CARD, LEAD AN EQUAL AND IF IT IS NOT COVERED DISCARD A LOSER. LATER YOU CAN DISCARD ANOTHER LOSER(S) ON THE ESTABLISHED EQUAL(S). THIS WAS, IN EFFECT, WHAT YOU DID WITH THE DIAMOND SUIT ON THIS HAND.

2. WHEN DISCARDING A LOSER ON AN EQUAL, DISCARD AN IMMEDIATE RATHER THAN AN EVENTUAL LOSER. CONSIDER THIS HAND. YOU MUST DISCARD A SPADE RATHER THAN A CLUB ON THE QUEEN OF DIAMONDS. IF YOU DISCARD A CLUB, WEST CAN WIN AND SHIFT TO A SPADE SCORING THREE TRICKS IN THAT SUIT. HOWEVER, IF YOU DISCARD A SPADE, THE CLUB CAN BE DISCARDED LATER AS YOU HAVE CONTROL OF THAT SUIT.

(64) DIAMONDS ARE A GIRL'S BEST FRIEND

East-West vulnerable
Dealer South

North
♠ 9 3
♡ 10 6 5
♢ A K Q 4 2
♣ 7 4 2

South
♠ A 10 6
♡ A K Q
♢ 9 8 7 3
♣ K 8 5

South	West	North	East
1 NT	3 ♠	3 NT	All Pass

Opening lead: ♠ 7

East plays the queen. Do you win this trick? What is your plan?

DIAMONDS ARE A GIRL'S BEST FRIEND (Solution)

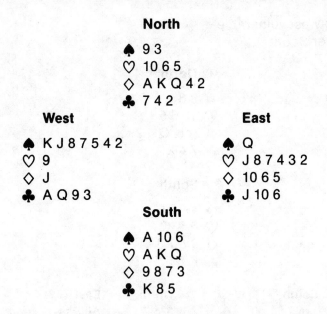

North
- ♠ 9 3
- ♡ 10 6 5
- ◇ A K Q 4 2
- ♣ 7 4 2

West
- ♠ K J 8 7 5 4 2
- ♡ 9
- ◇ J
- ♣ A Q 9 3

East
- ♠ Q
- ♡ J 8 7 4 3 2
- ◇ 10 6 5
- ♣ J 10 6

South
- ♠ A 10 6
- ♡ A K Q
- ◇ 9 8 7 3
- ♣ K 8 5

There is a small (very, very small) case for ducking the queen of spades. If East has all four diamonds along with the ace of clubs and a second spade you are better off if you duck.

To say this is a long shot is putting it mildly. West figures to have seven spades plus the ace of clubs for his vulnerable vs. non vulnerable intervention of a strong notrump opening.

The real danger is that East is going to shift to a club if you allow the queen of spades to hold. The opponents might just reel off four club tricks along with the queen of spades taking the first five tricks when you had nine tricks ready to go all along! Wonderful.

No, you should definitely WIN the first spade. But, did you notice the interior block in the diamond suit? In order to run the diamonds (if they break 3-1) you must underplay the nine-eight-seven beneath the ace-king-queen. This liberates the four to squash the three. How cozy. You score five diamonds, three hearts, and a spade.

KEY LESSON POINTERS

1. DON'T MAKE UNNECESSARY HOLD-UP PLAYS WHEN YOU HAVE ENOUGH TRICKS TO GUARANTEE YOUR CONTRACT AND A SHIFT TO ANOTHER SUIT COULD BE DEVASTATING.
2. WHEN RUNNING A LONG SUIT BE CAREFUL OF INTERIOR BLOCKAGE. THE TIPOFF IS WHEN THE SHORTER SIDE HAS HIGH INTERMEDIATE CARDS. GET THOSE OUT OF THE WAY EARLY!

(65) SPOTTING A JACK

Both sides vulnerable
Dealer South

North
♠ 4 3 2
♡ Q 10 3 2
◇ Q 3 2
♣ A K J

South
♠ K Q J
♡ A K 2
◇ A K 5 4
♣ Q 10 9

South	West	North	East
2 NT	Pass	6 NT	All Pass

Opening lead: ♠ 10

East wins the ace and returns a spade. You play a third spade and East discards a club. Next you run off three rounds of clubs and West discards a spade on third club.

Hoping for a 3-3 diamond break you play off your three top diamonds. No luck. West discards a spade on the third diamond. How do you plan to play the heart suit?

SPOTTING A JACK (Solution)

North

♠ 4 3 2
♡ Q 10 3 2
♢ Q 3 2
♣ A K J

West

♠ 10 9 8 7 6
♡ J 9 8 7
♢ 7 6
♣ 3 2

East

♠ A 5
♡ 6 3
♢ J 10 9 8
♣ 8 7 6 5 4

South

♠ K Q J
♡ A K 2
♢ A K 5 4
♣ Q 10 9

You should plan to play the king-ace of hearts and lead a low heart to the ten. West has turned up with five spades, (you knew that when East discarded on the third round of spades) two clubs and two diamonds. Presto! West has four hearts and East only two. See how much fun this is?

KEY LESSON POINTERS

1. WHEN PLAYING CONTRACTS IN WHICH YOU FIND YOURSELF WITH ALL THE TRICKS BUT ONE, IT USUALLY PAYS TO CASH YOUR TRICKS IN THE FOLLOWING ORDER:
    A. CASH TRICKS IN SUITS WHERE YOU HAVE ZERO CHANCE TO GAIN EXTRA TRICKS—NON-THREAT SUITS. (SPADES AND CLUBS)
    B. SAVE ANY SUIT WHICH HAS A TWO-WAY POSSIBILITY UNTIL THE VERY END. (HEARTS, AS YOU CAN EITHER PLAY ACE-KING-QUEEN OR ACE-KING-TEN.)
    C. WHICHEVER SUITS ARE LEFT SHOULD BE PLAYED IN BETWEEN. (DIAMONDS SHOULD BE PLAYED AFTER THE BLACK SUITS—BUT BEFORE THE HEARTS.)
2. THE REASON IT PAYS TO CASH TRICKS IN THIS ORDER IS THAT YOU GIVE THE OPPONENTS EVERY OPPORTUNITY TO MAKE AN "UNFORTUNATE" DISCARD. UNFORTUNATE FOR THEM, THAT IS.

(66) DON'T LET THAT MAN IN!

North-South vulnerable
Dealer South

North
- ♠ K Q 4
- ♡ 2
- ◇ A Q 8 6 5 4
- ♣ 6 5 2

South
- ♠ A J 7
- ♡ A Q 9 8 3
- ◇ J 2
- ♣ A 9 3

South	West	North	East
1 ♡	2 ♣	2 ◇	Pass
2 NT	Pass	3 NT	All Pass

Opening lead: ♣ K

You duck the opening lead but win the club queen continuation, East shedding a small spade.

You lead the jack of diamonds at trick three and West covers. How do you continue?

DON'T LET THAT MAN IN! (Solution)

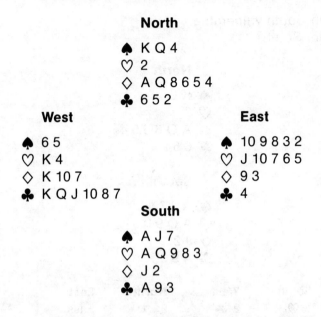

North

♠ K Q 4
♡ 2
◇ A Q 8 6 5 4
♣ 6 5 2

West

♠ 6 5
♡ K 4
◇ K 10 7
♣ K Q J 10 8 7

East

♠ 10 9 8 3 2
♡ J 10 7 6 5
◇ 9 3
♣ 4

South

♠ A J 7
♡ A Q 9 8 3
◇ J 2
♣ A 9 3

Obviously you can't duck the king of diamonds. (You did read the title above the hand, didn't you?) West is ready with an avalanche of good clubs.

No you must win the ace of diamonds, cross to the ace of spades and lead the deuce of diamonds. Assuming West follows with a low diamond, insert the EIGHT. If East wins, the diamonds have divided and you have ten tricks—five diamonds, three spades, a heart and a club.

If West plays either the nine or ten of diamonds on the second round of the suit, win the queen and play a third diamond hoping East wins the trick. If he does, you are home once again with ten tricks.

If West wins the third diamond—oh well. Finally, if West shows out on the second round of diamonds, duck the trick into East. If East returns a heart you are in trouble. Play the ace and hope West has a singleton king or that East has the king. Now back to dummy with a spade and play queen and a diamond, establishing the suit..

Now all you have to do is sweat out the king of hearts. If East has it, no more problem—if West has it—no more tricks!

KEY LESSON POINTERS

1. WHEN FACED WITH THE PROBLEM OF KEEPING ONE HAND OFF LEAD AIM ALL YOUR FINESSES INTO THE OTHER HAND.
2. WATCH THE SPOT CARDS CLOSELY IN THE SUIT YOU ARE ESTABLISHING. SOMETIMES FINESSES CAN BE MADE WITH SMALLER CARDS. TAKE A GOOD LOOK AT THE DIAMOND SUIT IN THIS PROBLEM TO APPRECIATE THE VALUE OF THE EIGHT OF DIAMONDS.

(67) NOT SO LUCKY YOU

Both sides vulnerable
Dealer South

North

♠ 5 4 3
♡ 8 6 4
♢ 9 6 2
♣ A K 7 4

South

♠ A K Q J 10
♡ A K 7 5
♢ Q J
♣ 6 2

South	West	North	East
1 ♠	Pass	1 NT	Pass
3 ♡	Pass	3 ♠	Pass
4 ♠	All Pass		

Opening lead: ♢ K

West continues with the ace and ten of diamonds, East following. Plan the play.

NOT SO LUCKY YOU (Solution)

North

♠ 5 4 3
♡ 8 6 4
◇ 9 6 2
♣ A K 7 4

West	East
West	**East**
♠ 9 8 7	♠ 6 2
♡ J 9 3 2	♡ Q 10
◇ A K 10 5	◇ 8 7 4 3
♣ 9 8	♣ Q J 10 5 3

South

♠ A K Q J 10
♡ A K 7 5
◇ Q J
♣ 6 2

You have lost two diamond tricks, and your only other loser(s) is in the heart suit.

If the suit divides 3-3 you will be O.K., but what if hearts divide normally, 4-2?

You must assume a 4-2 division and see if you can do anything about it. With no discards available for that lousy fourth heart you must plan to trump it in dummy.

The problem is, you only have low trumps in dummy and some one might overtrump. Look at the heart position.

If you play ace-king and a third heart, West can win and play a fourth heart allowing East to overtrump dummy. If, on the other hand, you draw two rounds of trumps before conceding a heart, West can play a third trump and frustrate you once again.

The answer—when you have to trump a fourth card LOW in dummy—is to first duck a card in the suit, then draw two rounds of trumps and finally trump your fourth card in dummy.

KEY LESSON POINTERS

1. ASSUMING YOU MUST TRUMP A FOURTH ROUND LOSER
   (a) WITH A HIGH TRUMP:
   CASH YOUR WINNERS IN THE SUIT AND THEN CONCEDE WHAT-EVER LOSERS YOU MAY HAVE PRIOR TO RUFFING.
   (b) WITH A LOW TRUMP:
   USE THE DUCKING—THEN DRAWING TWO TRUMPS—TECHNIQUE DESCRIBED ABOVE.

(68)   AN ACE AND A QUEEN MISSING

East-West vulnerable
Dealer South

North

♠ A 7
♡ K 4 3 2
◇ 9 8 7 6
♣ A Q J

South

♠ K Q J 10 9 8
♡ A J 5
◇ K 10
♣ K 3

South	West	North	East
1 ♠	Pass	2 NT	Pass
4 ♣*	Pass	4 ♠**	Pass
6 ♠	All Pass		

  *Gerber—asking for aces.
**Two aces

Opening lead: ♣ 10

Plan the play.

AN ACE AND A QUEEN MISSING (Solution)

North

♠ A 7
♡ K 4 3 2
♢ 9 8 7 6
♣ A Q J

West

♠ 5 4 3
♡ Q 8
♢ A J 5
♣ 10 9 8 7 6

East

♠ 6 2
♡ 10 9 7 6
♢ Q 4 3 2
♣ 5 4 2

South

♠ K Q J 10 9 8
♡ A J 5
♢ K 10
♣ K 3

You have a possible loser in hearts along with two possible losers in diamonds, but, you do have one extra winner in clubs. All in all two possible losers and eleven top tricks—six spades, three clubs, and two hearts.

There are finesses available in both red suits. Which one to take first?

In these two-suited finesse option hands, you must try to look for a way to COMBINE your chances and not put all of your eggs in one basket.

Here you can do just that. Win the club lead in dummy (say) and draw the necessary trumps discarding diamonds from the table. Next, try the ace-king of hearts hoping for the queen to drop. If it does, (it does!) your troubles are over as a diamond can be discarded on a club.

If the queen of hearts does not drop, discard the jack of hearts on the club and lead toward the king of diamonds.

KEY LESSON POINTERS

1. WITH TWO FINESSES AVAILABLE, EITHER ONE OF WHICH WILL GIVE YOU YOUR CONTRACT, TRY TO COMBINE YOUR CHANCES.
2. WHEN COMBINING CHANCES IN TWO SUITS, ONE MISSING A QUEEN, THE OTHER AN ACE, (WITH ONE SIDE DISCARD AVAILABLE AND ONLY ONE TRICK THAT CAN AFFORD TO BE LOST), PLAY THE ACE-KING OF THE QUEEN SUIT. IF THE QUEEN HAS NOT DROPPED, TAKE THE DISCARD IN THAT SUIT AND THEN LEAD UP TO THE KING IN THE OTHER SUIT.

(69) SOLID SUIT

North-South vulnerable
Dealer East

North
♠ K 6 5 4 3
♡ 5
♢ 10 9 8 5
♣ A K J

South
♠ 2
♡ A K Q J 10 9 8
♢ J 4 3 2
♣ 2

East	South	West	North
Pass	4 ♡	All Pass	

Opening lead: ♠ Q

You play low from dummy, and East plays the nine. At trick two West shifts to the five of clubs. Plan the play.

SOLID SUIT (Solution)

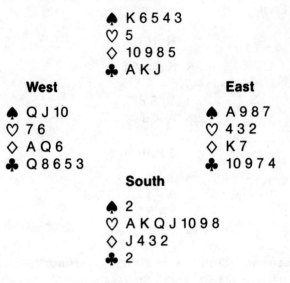

North

♠ K 6 5 4 3
♡ 5
◇ 10 9 8 5
♣ A K J

West

♠ Q J 10
♡ 7 6
◇ A Q 6
♣ Q 8 6 5 3

East

♠ A 9 8 7
♡ 4 3 2
◇ K 7
♣ 10 9 7 4

South

♠ 2
♡ A K Q J 10 9 8
◇ J 4 3 2
♣ 2

What is going on? Hard to tell, but what about losers?

You have lost a spade and you have three quick diamond losers. Fortunately that suit has not been attacked.

One diamond discard on a club won't do any good so you have to go for it! Put in the jack of clubs! If it loses, down two. If it works, a vulnerable game!

Why didn't West shift to a diamond? Haven't your opponents ever made a mistake against you before? Well, they just have.

KEY LESSON POINTERS

1. KEEP THAT LOSER COUNT IN MIND AT ALL TIMES. PLAYS IN OTHER SUITS DEPEND UPON IT.

2. IN A CONTRACT OF THREE HEARTS, A CLUB FINESSE WOULD BE JUST ABOUT THE SILLIEST PLAY YOU COULD MAKE. YOU DO HAVE NINE TRICKS, YOU KNOW. NO POINT IN CONDENSING THEM INTO EIGHT JUST TO TRY FOR AN OVERTRICK.

3. MAKE YOUR "BIG" PLAYS WHEN YOUR CONTRACT IS INVOLVED, NOT FOR OVERTRICKS—UNLESS YOU ARE 99.9% SURE YOU HAVE THE HAND PEGGED.

(70) HOLDING ON

East-West vulnerable
Dealer South

North
♠ K 2
♡ J 2
◇ 5 4 3 2
♣ K 7 4 3 2

South
♠ A J 10 9 5
♡ A K Q 10 6
◇ 10
♣ A 5

South	West	North	East
1 ♠	Pass	1 NT	Pass
3 ♡	Pass	3 ♠	Pass
4 ♡	Pass	4 ♠	All Pass

Opening lead: ◇ K

East signals with the nine and West continues with the queen of diamonds, East playing the seven. Plan the play.

HOLDING ON (Solution)

North

♠ K 2
♡ J 2
◇ 5 4 3 2
♣ K 7 4 3 2

West

♠ Q 8 7 4
♡ 9 7
◇ K Q J 6
♣ J 8 6

East

♠ 6 3
♡ 8 5 4 3
◇ A 9 8 7
♣ Q 10 9

South

♠ A J 10 9 5
♡ A K Q 10 5
◇ 10
♣ A 5

Ruff the second diamond and play the king-ace of spades leaving two spades outstanding. You can afford to lose two trump tricks but cannot afford to be shortened again. (Spades may be 4-2). Play out your heart and club winners allowing the opponents to score their two trump tricks.

KEY LESSON POINTERS

1. WITH A SOLID SIDE SUIT AND NO SIDE LOSERS, ASK YOURSELF HOW MANY TRUMP TRICKS YOU CAN AFFORD TO LOSE.

2. WHEN THERE IS A DANGER OF BEING SHORTENED IN THE TRUMP SUIT TO A POINT WHERE ONE OPPONENT MAY WIND UP WITH MORE TRUMPS THAN YOU, CONSIDER THE POSSIBILITY OF CASHING YOUR HIGH TRUMPS, DISDAINING ANY FINESSE, ALLOWING THE OPPONENTS TO MAKE WHATEVER TRUMPS THEY HAVE LEFT—SEPARATELY —PROVIDING THEY WON'T TAKE ENOUGH TRICKS TO DEFEAT YOU.

3. CONSIDER THIS HAND. YOU HAVE BEEN SHORTENED DOWN TO FOUR TRUMPS, AND YOU CAN AFFORD TO LOSE TWO TRUMP TRICKS. WITH A NORMAL 4-2 TRUMP DIVISION, THE OPPONENTS REMAIN WITH TWO TRUMPS AFTER YOU SCORE THE ACE-KING. YOU ALSO REMAIN WITH TWO TRUMPS, BUT IT IS YOUR LEAD. YOU CAN PLAY GOOD HEARTS AND CLUBS AND CANNOT POSSIBLY LOSE MORE THAN TWO MORE TRICKS. HAD YOU FINESSED SPADES AND HAD IT LOST, A SUBSEQUENT DIAMOND RETURN ALONG WITH A 4-2 SPADE DIVISION WOULD HAVE RUINED YOU.

(71) TOO HIGH?

Both sides vulnerable
Dealer West

North
♠ A J 8 7
♡ K J
♢ A K J 10
♣ 10 9 8

South
♠ Q 10 9 4 3
♡ 7 6
♢ Q 9 8
♣ 4 3 2

West	North	East	South
Pass	1 NT	Pass	2 ♠
Pass	3 ♠	All Pass	

Opening lead: ♣ K

West continues with the queen and jack of clubs, East signalling first with the seven and then with the five and six.

At trick four West shifts to a low heart. The ball is back in your court. Which heart do you play?

TOO HIGH? (Solution)

North

♠ A J 8 7
♡ K J
♢ A K J 10
♣ 10 9 8

West

♠ K 2
♡ Q 10 4 3
♢ 7 6 5 4
♣ K Q J

East

♠ 6 5
♡ A 9 8 5 2
♢ 3 2
♣ A 7 6 5

South

♠ Q 10 9 4 3
♡ 7 6
♢ Q 9 8
♣ 4 3 2

Don't play too quickly. It is not a guess. Think about the bidding plus what has happened so far.

West is a passed hand and has turned up with 6 points in clubs. (East certainly has the club ace judging from his high-low signal.)

Regardless of what you do in hearts you are still going to have to find the king of spades with West. As long as you need the king of spades in the West hand to make your contract, ASSUME IT IS THERE. Now see if that doesn't help you in hearts. If West really does have the king of spades, he cannot possibly have the ace of hearts or else he would have opened the bidding. Play the jack of hearts.

KEY LESSON POINTERS

1. WHEN THE OPPONENTS "PUT IT TO YOU" EARLY IN THE HAND, YOU MIGHT BE FORCED TO MAKE SOME ASSUMPTIONS AS TO THE LOCATION OF OTHER MISSING KEY HONORS. THIS MIGHT HELP YOU PLACE HONOR CARDS IN THE SUIT THEY HAVE JUST LED.

   IF, IN ORDER TO MAKE THE CONTRACT, YOU NEED ANOTHER CARD IN ANOTHER SUIT WELL PLACED, ASSUME IT IS WELL PLACED AND SEE IF THAT DOES NOT HELP YOU WITH THE SUIT THAT IS BEING LED.

   IF, ON THE OTHER HAND, YOU CAN MAKE THE CONTRACT EVEN IF ANOTHER KEY HONOR IS POORLY PLACED, ASSUME IT IS POORLY PLACED AND PLAY ACCORDINGLY IN THE SUIT THAT IS BEING LED.

2. ONE OF THE BIGGEST CLUES YOU HAVE WHEN IT COMES TO LOCATING MISSING HONORS IS THE ORIGINAL PASS. WHATEVER ELSE, DON'T FORGET THAT!

(72) WHO HAS IT?

East-West vulnerable
Dealer North

North

♠ Q 10
♡ Q 7 3 2
◇ A J 10 9
♣ K Q 4

South

♠ 4 3
♡ A K 10 8 6 5
◇ K 7 2
♣ 7 3

North	East	South	West
1 ◇	Pass	1 ♡	Pass
2 ♡	Pass	4 ♡	All Pass

Opening lead: ♣ J

You cover with the queen and East wins the ace and returns the five of clubs to the nine and king. You lead a trump to the king and all follow. How do you play the diamonds?

WHO HAS IT? (Solution)

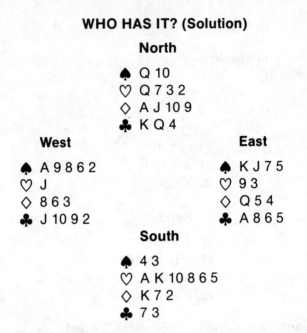

North
- ♠ Q 10
- ♡ Q 7 3 2
- ◇ A J 10 9
- ♣ K Q 4

West
- ♠ A 9 8 6 2
- ♡ J
- ◇ 8 6 3
- ♣ J 10 9 2

East
- ♠ K J 7 5
- ♡ 9 3
- ◇ Q 5 4
- ♣ A 8 6 5

South
- ♠ 4 3
- ♡ A K 10 8 6 5
- ◇ K 7 2
- ♣ 7 3

You don't! Why play diamonds forcing yourself to guess when you can force the diamond play from the opponents?

Enter dummy with the queen of hearts and ruff the last club. Now simply exit with a spade, your evenly divided suit.

After cashing two spade tricks the opponents will either have to attack diamonds, eliminating the possible loser, or give you a ruff and a sluff allowing you to ruff in dummy and discard a diamond from your hand.

KEY LESSON POINTERS

1. WHEN YOU HAVE A SUIT WITH A TWO-WAY GUESS (DIAMONDS) AND A SUIT THAT IS EVENLY DIVIDED BETWEEN YOUR HAND AND DUMMY (SPADES) USE THE EVENLY DIVIDED SUIT TO FORCE A LEAD IN THE OTHER SUIT. HOWEVER, IN ORDER TO DO THAT, YOU MUST DRAW TRUMPS LEAVING TRUMPS ON BOTH SIDES AND ELIMINATE THE FOURTH SUIT (CLUBS) FROM BOTH HANDS BEFORE EXITING WITH A SPADE.

2. WHEN THE OPPONENTS GIVE YOU A RUFF AND SLUFF, IT IS ALMOST ALWAYS RIGHT TO RUFF IN THE HAND THAT IS LONGER IN THE SUIT YOU WANTED THEM TO LEAD. IN THAT CASE YOU CAN DISCARD A LOSER FROM THE SHORTER SIDE OF YOUR TOUCHY SUIT.

   CONSIDER THIS HAND. IF, AFTER YOU STRIP THE HAND AND EXIT WITH A SPADE, THE OPPONENTS CASH TWO SPADES AND PLAY A THIRD YOU MUST RUFF IN DUMMY (THE LONGER HAND IN DIAMONDS) AND DISCARD A DIAMOND FROM YOUR HAND. IF YOU DO IT THE OTHER WAY AROUND YOU ARE STILL FACED WITH A DIAMOND GUESS. FOR SHAME.

(73) LUCKY SEVEN

East-West vulnerable
Dealer North

North

♠ A Q 10 4 2
♡ A 4 3
♢ A 3
♣ 9 4 2

South

♠ 5
♡ K 7 5
♢ K J 10 9 2
♣ J 8 6 3

North	East	South	West
1 ♠	Pass	1 NT	All Pass

Opening lead: ♡ J

If you are one of those players that would have rebid two spades with the North hand, do not admit it in public. You should have six cards in your major suit to rebid it after a one notrump response.

In any case this is a play problem. What is your plan?

LUCKY SEVEN (Solution)

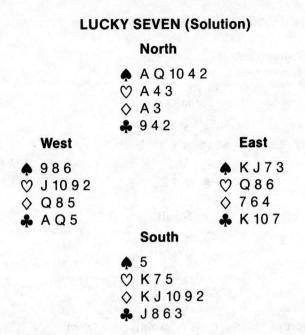

North
♠ A Q 10 4 2
♡ A 4 3
♢ A 3
♣ 9 4 2

West
♠ 9 8 6
♡ J 10 9 2
♢ Q 8 5
♣ A Q 5

East
♠ K J 7 3
♡ Q 8 6
♢ 7 6 4
♣ K 10 7

South
♠ 5
♡ K 7 5
♢ K J 10 9 2
♣ J 8 6 3

First things first. Count your sure tricks OUTSIDE of your best suit. Your best suit is diamonds and you have three sure tricks outside of diamonds, two hearts and a spade.

Now you know how many tricks you need from your best suit. FOUR. What could be simpler? Win the ACE of hearts and play the ace and a diamond to the jack. Assuming this loses you still have the king of hearts as a hand entry to your established diamonds—and providing you don't get greedy and take an unnecessary spade finesse,—if West shifts to that suit,—you have seven sure tricks. Four diamonds, two hearts and one spade. (If the spade finesse loses you have no entry back to the spade ace!)

KEY LESSON POINTERS

1. AT NOTRUMP CONTRACTS COUNT SURE TRICKS OUTSIDE OF YOUR BEST SUIT. THIS WILL TELL YOU HOW MANY TRICKS YOU NEED TO DEVELOP IN YOUR BEST SUIT.
2. WHEN PLANNING TO DEVELOP A SUIT, MAKE SURE THAT YOU RETAIN AS MANY SIDE ENTRIES TO THAT HAND AS POSSIBLE. ON THIS HAND IT WOULD HAVE BEEN DISASTROUS TO WIN THE OPENING LEAD IN THE CLOSED HAND.
3. WHEN PLAYING A COMBINATION OF CARDS THAT IS DIVIDED 5-2 BETWEEN YOUR HAND AND DUMMY, IT IS ALMOST ALWAYS RIGHT EITHER TO BEGIN WITH THE HIGH CARD FROM THE SHORT SIDE, OR TO LEAD TOWARDS IT IN ORDER NOT TO BLOCK THE SUIT. FOR EXAMPLE, WITH AKxxx FACING Jx, LEAD TOWARD THE JACK WITH KJxxx FACING Qx, LEAD TOWARD THE QUEEN (BEST); IF THAT IS NOT POSSIBLE, LEAD THE QUEEN.

(74) WHAT A FIT

East-West vulnerable
Dealer North

North
♠ 8 7 3 2
♡ K J 2
◇ A J 10
♣ Q 10 2

South
♠ 5
♡ A 9 3
◇ K Q 9 2
♣ A K J 9 6

North	East	South	West
Pass	Pass	1 ♣	Pass
2 NT	Pass	3 ◇	Pass
3 ♡*	Pass	4 ♣	Pass
4 ◇	Pass	4 ♡	Pass
5 ♣	Pass	6 ♣	All Pass

*Strength in hearts plus weakness in spades

Opening lead: ♠ K

West continues with the ace of spades. Plan the play.

WHAT A FIT! (Solution)

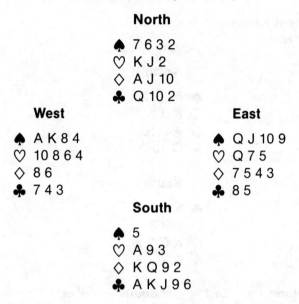

North
- ♠ 7 6 3 2
- ♡ K J 2
- ◇ A J 10
- ♣ Q 10 2

West
- ♠ A K 8 4
- ♡ 10 8 6 4
- ◇ 8 6
- ♣ 7 4 3

East
- ♠ Q J 10 9
- ♡ Q 7 5
- ◇ 7 5 4 3
- ♣ 8 5

South
- ♠ 5
- ♡ A 9 3
- ◇ K Q 9 2
- ♣ A K J 9 6

The only possible loser is a heart and even that might be avoided by means of a finesse. But why finesse? Why not discard it on a trump?

After ruffing the second spade, play the ace and a club to the ten. If trumps are 4-1, draw the remaining trumps and eventually fall back on the heart finesse.

However, if trumps are 3-2, ruff a spade in your hand, cross to dummy with the jack or ten of diamonds, and ruff dummy's last spade with your last trump. Return to dummy with the king of hearts, and discard your losing nine of hearts on dummy's queen of clubs. Your hand is now high.

KEY LESSON POINTERS

1. WHEN PLAYING A 5-3 TRUMP FIT, AN EXTRA TRUMP TRICK CAN BE MANAGED IF YOU ARRANGE TO TRUMP THREE TIMES IN THE LONG HAND. BE SURE YOU HAVE ENOUGH DUMMY ENTRIES TO PULL OFF THIS TYPE OF PLAY.

2. IT IS IMPORTANT TO NOTICE THAT ON THIS HAND YOU HAD THE LUXURY OF FIRST DRAWING TWO ROUNDS OF TRUMPS TO CHECK OUT A POSSIBLE 4-1 TRUMP DIVISION. HAD YOU FOUND IT, YOU WOULD HAVE HAD TO ABANDON YOUR DUMMY REVERSAL. RUFFING TWICE IN THE LONG HAND, LET ALONE THREE TIMES, WOULD HAVE RESULTED IN THE LOSS OF A TRUMP TRICK.

3. REMEMBER A 3-2 TRUMP DIVISION OCCURS 68% OF THE TIME, SO EVEN IF YOU CAN'T AFFORD THE LUXURY OF DRAWING TWO ROUNDS OF TRUMPS, A DUMMY REVERSAL MAY WELL BE YOUR BEST CHANCE. CERTAINLY BETTER THAN A FINESSE (50%) OR HOPING A SIDE SUIT BREAKS 3-3 (36%).

(75)   NO SECOND CHANCES

Both sides vulnerable
Dealer South

North
- ♠ K 9 7 6
- ♡ K 2
- ◇ A 5 3
- ♣ J 7 4 2

South
- ♠ A 4 3
- ♡ 8 4 3
- ◇ K J 10 4
- ♣ A K Q

South	West	North	East
1 NT	Pass	2 ♣*	Pass
2 ◇**	Pass	3 NT	All Pass

*Stayman—asking for a four card major.

**No four card major.

Opening lead: ♠ Queen

What is your plan?

NO SECOND CHANCES (Solution)

North

♠ K 9 7 6
♡ K 2
◇ A 5 3
♣ J 7 4 2

<table>
<tr><td>West</td><td>East</td></tr>
<tr><td>♠ Q J 10 8</td><td>♠ 5 2</td></tr>
<tr><td>♡ Q J 9</td><td>♡ A 10 7 6 5</td></tr>
<tr><td>◇ Q 8 7 2</td><td>◇ 9 6</td></tr>
<tr><td>♣ 5 3</td><td>♣ 10 9 8 6</td></tr>
</table>

South

♠ A 4 3
♡ 8 4 3
◇ K J 10 4
♣ A K Q

You start with eight sure tricks, four clubs, two diamonds and two spades. You were fortunate not to get a heart lead and you don't want to have to put up with one later from West, that is.

It is easy enough to set up your ninth trick in diamonds but you must be careful to finesse diamonds into EAST, the player who cannot hurt you with a heart switch.

Win the ace of spades and run the jack of diamonds. If it loses you have nine tricks and if it wins you may make more if the diamonds come down or if the ace of hearts is with West.

Incidentally, it wouldn't be a bad idea to unblock your clubs before chewing up all of dummy's entries!

KEY LESSON POINTERS

1. WHEN YOU HAVE A VULNERABLE SUIT THAT CAN ONLY BE ATTACKED PROFITABLY FROM ONE DEFENDER, THAT DEFENDER IS KNOWN AS THE DANGER HAND. HIS PARTNER IS THE NON-DANGER HAND.

2. ONE TENDS TO LIVE A HEALTHIER LIFE IF ONE TAKES FINESSES INTO THE NON-DANGER HAND WHENEVER POSSIBLE. DO IT THE OTHER WAY AROUND, AND YOUR PARTNER BECOMES THE DANGER HAND!

3. THE DANGER HAND IDEA OFTEN FORCES YOU TO PLAY A SUIT DIFFERENTLY THAN YOU WOULD LIKE. FOR INSTANCE, WITH THIS DIAMOND COMBINATION THE BEST PLAY FOR FOUR TRICKS IS ACE AND LOW TO THE TEN. HOWEVER ONE SELDOM PLAYS SUITS IN ISOLATION. THE VULNERABILITY OF THE HEART POSITION AFFECTS THE MANAGEMENT OF THE DIAMOND SUIT.

(76) LUCKY YOU

Both sides vulnerable
Dealer South

North

♠ J 4 3
♡ 8 6 4
◇ 9 6 2
♣ A K 7 2

South

♠ A K Q 10 9
♡ A K 7 2
◇ J 8
♣ 6 3

South	West	North	East
1 ♠	Pass	2 ♠	Pass
4 ♠	All Pass		

Opening lead: ◇ K

West cashes two top diamonds and leads a third diamond to East's ten. Plan the play.

LUCKY YOU (Solution)

North
♠ J 4 3
♡ 8 6 4
♢ 9 6 2
♣ A K 7 2

West
♠ 8 7
♡ J 9 5 3
♢ A K 4 3
♣ J 9 8

East
♠ 6 5 2
♡ Q 10
♢ Q 10 7 5
♣ Q 10 5 4

South
♠ A K Q 10 9
♡ A K 7 2
♢ J 8
♣ 6 3

You have lost two diamond tricks and your only other losers are in hearts.

When you have four cards in your hand opposite three cards in the dummy, as you do in hearts, you must make provision for that fourth card in case the suit does not break 3-3 as it does for everyone else.

What you might have to do with that fourth card is trump it in the dummy. If you are blessed, dummy will have a high trump; if not, you will have to trump it low.

In this example you are blessed. You have a high trump in dummy. Your play is to ruff the third diamond and immediately play ace-king and third heart. Win any return, say a club, cross to your hand with a trump and ruff your fourth heart with the jack of spades. Now return to your hand drawing trumps and you have made your contract.

KEY LESSON POINTERS

1. DO NOT OVERLOOK FOURTH CARDS IN SUITS THAT ARE DIVIDED 4-3 WITH THE FOUR CARD SUIT IN THE LONG TRUMP HAND. THAT FOURTH CARD WON'T GO AWAY. YOU HAVE GOT TO FIGURE OUT WHAT TO DO WITH IT.
2. IF YOU ARE BLESSED WITH A HIGH TRUMP IN DUMMY, TRUMP THE FOURTH CARD IN DUMMY AFTER YOU HAVE GIVEN UP ANY TRICKS YOU MUST LOSE IN THE SUIT. (SEE HAND #67)
3. IF YOU HAVE NO SIDE LOSERS IN THE SUIT (A K Qx FACING xxx) DRAW AS MANY TRUMPS AS POSSIBLE BEFORE TRYING TO TRUMP THE FOURTH CARD IN DUMMY.

(77)   SMALL SLAM

Both sides vulnerable
Dealer South

North

♠ K Q 2
♡ K 6 4 3
◇ A Q 7
♣ 4 3 2

South

♠ A J 6
♡ A 7 2
◇ K J 10 5
♣ A K J

South	West	North	East
2 NT	Pass	6 NT	All Pass

Opening lead: ♠ 10

What is your general plan?

SMALL SLAM (Solution)

North

♠ K Q 2
♡ K 6 4 3
♢ A Q 7
♣ 4 3 2

West

♠ 10 9 8 7
♡ J 8 5
♢ 6 3 2
♣ Q 10 6

East

♠ 5 4 3
♡ Q 10 9
♢ 9 8 4
♣ 9 8 7 5

South

♠ A J 6
♡ A 7 2
♢ K J 10 5
♣ A K J

You have eleven top tricks with chances of a twelfth trick in two suits, hearts and clubs.

If hearts divide 3-3 or the club finesse is right you make your slam. Can you combine your chances? Yes.

If you simply DUCK a heart in both hands, win the probable club return and then test the hearts by playing ace-king you will see if they break 3-3. If they do not, fall back on the club finesse.

KEY LESSON POINTERS

1. TO RETAIN CONTROL OF AN ACE-KING SUIT WHICH YOU ARE ESTABLISHING, IT IS USUALLY RIGHT TO DUCK ONE ROUND OF THE SUIT. LATER YOU CAN PLAY THE ACE-KING TO SEE HOW THE SUIT HAS DIVIDED. IF YOU PLAY THE ACE-KING AND THEN A SMALL ONE, AND SOMEONE HAS FOUR CARDS IN THE SUIT, THAT SOMEONE WILL SIMPLY CASH TWO TRICKS.

2. AVOID FINESSES IN EQUAL LENGTH SUITS (CLUBS). IN GENERAL, WORK WITH UNEQUAL LENGTH SUITS THAT OFFER AN OPPORTUNITY FOR LONG SUIT OR EXTRA TRICK ESTABLISHMENT.

(78) THE BRIGHT SIDE

Both sides vulnerable
Dealer North

North
♠ A Q 5
♡ 10 8 5
◇ 7 3
♣ A Q 6 5 4

South
♠ K J 4 2
♡ K J 4
◇ A J 5
♣ J 10 9

North	East	South	West
1 ♣	Pass	2 NT	Pass
3 NT	All Pass		

Opening lead: ◇ 6

East plays the queen which you allow to hold. (Of course you know why.) East continues with the nine of diamonds which you cover with the jack and West wins with the king. West returns the ten of diamonds, you discard a heart from dummy, East follows with the four and you win.

You run the jack of clubs which loses to East (of course) and East returns a low heart (of course). Which heart do you play?

THE BRIGHT SIDE (Solution)

North

♠ A Q 5
♡ 10 8 5
♢ 7 3
♣ A Q 6 5 4

West

♠ 9 8
♡ Q 6 3
♢ K 10 8 6 2
♣ 8 3 2

East

♠ 10 7 6 3
♡ A 9 7 2
♢ Q 9 4
♣ K 7

South

♠ K J 4 2
♡ K J 4
♢ A J 5
♣ J 10 9

Before worrying about which heart to play you should know why you ducked the diamond at trick one, and how the diamonds are divided.

You ducked the diamond because the club finesse is going into East and you didn't want East to have any diamonds left in case he had the king of clubs.

East's return of the nine of diamonds indicates a three card holding. With FOUR diamonds East normally returns his LOWEST remaining diamond.

So—you have lost three tricks and you KNOW that West has two established diamonds ready to go. If West has the ace of hearts you cannot make the hand regardless of which heart you play, so you must assume East has the ace of hearts. Play the KING.

KEY LESSON POINTERS

1. WATCH THIRD HAND'S RETURN OF HIS PARTNER'S SUIT TO DETERMINE THE ORIGINAL DIVISION OF THE SUIT.
2. WHEN A KJ COMBINATION IN EITHER YOUR HAND OR DUMMY IS BEING LED THROUGH, AND THE PLAYER SITTING OVER THE K J HAS THE SETTING TRICKS IN ANOTHER SUIT, YOU MIGHT AS WELL PLAY THE KING. YOU ARE NOT GOING TO MAKE THE HAND IF THE ACE IS IN THE HAND WITH THE SETTING TRICKS, SO PLAY THE PARTNER FOR THE ACE. GIVE YOURSELF A BREAK. YOU DESERVE IT.
3. YES, WEST CAN DEFEAT THE CONTRACT BY SHIFTING TO A LOW HEART AT TRICK THREE—PROVIDING EAST WINS AND RETURNS A HEART, NOT A DIAMOND, AS HE SHOULD.

(79) WHAT CAN POSSIBLY HAPPEN?

Neither side vulnerable
Dealer North

North
♠ K Q J
♡ K 5 4
♢ A K 7 4
♣ 4 3 2

South
♠ 7 6 3
♡ A J 9 8 3 2
♢ J
♣ K 6 5

North	East	South	West
1 NT	Pass	4 ♡	All Pass

Opening lead: ♣ Q

East wins the ace and returns the seven of clubs. Plan the play.

WHAT CAN POSSIBLY HAPPEN? (Solution)

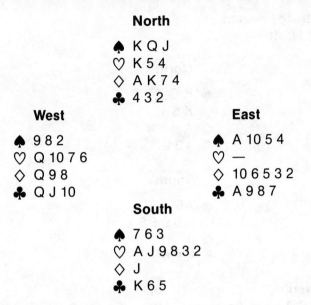

North
- ♠ K Q J
- ♡ K 5 4
- ◇ A K 7 4
- ♣ 4 3 2

West
- ♠ 9 8 2
- ♡ Q 10 7 6
- ◇ Q 9 8
- ♣ Q J 10

East
- ♠ A 10 5 4
- ♡ —
- ◇ 10 6 5 3 2
- ♣ A 9 8 7

South
- ♠ 7 6 3
- ♡ A J 9 8 3 2
- ◇ J
- ♣ K 6 5

Things look pretty rosy. You can discard your losing club on a top diamond and you have only a spade and perhaps a trump to lose.

But wait! When things look TOO good ask yourself what can possibly go wrong? In this case the only thing that can go wrong is all four trumps in one hand.

Well, if that is all that can go wrong, take out a little insurance. Remember, you can afford to lose one trump trick but not two.

Win the king of clubs and play the ACE of hearts. If everyone follows, cross to the king of hearts. Assuming hearts are 3-1 and the queen is outstanding, play off the top diamonds, discarding a club, conceding a spade and a trump to the bad guys.

However, if someone shows out on the ace of hearts, you must proceed with a bit more caution. Say, for example, that West shows out. Fine. Cross to the king of hearts, discard the losing club and lead up to the jack of hearts. You only lose one trump trick that way.

Say that East shows out—as in the diagram. Fine. Play the eight of hearts which West must cover, win with the king, discard the club and concede a heart to West's queen.

KEY LESSON POINTERS

1. WHEN THINGS LOOK ROSIEST, ASK YOURSELF WHAT CAN POSSIBLY GO WRONG—THEN TRY TO CATER TO THAT POSSIBILITY.
2. WITH KJxxxx FACING A9x, or KJxxx FACING A9xx, START WITH THE KING OR START BY LEADING LOW TO THE KING TO INSURE THE LOSS OF ONLY ONE TRICK.

(80) A PAIR OF NINES

East-West vulnerable
Dealer West

North

♠ 5 4 3
♡ J 9 8 2
♢ J 7 4
♣ J 9 2

South

♠ A K Q J 9 2
♡ 10 7
♢ 6
♣ A Q 10 5

West	North	East	South
Pass	Pass	1 ♢	4 ♠
All Pass			

Opening lead: ♢ K

East signals with the ten of diamonds and West continues with the deuce to East's ace. Plan the play.

A PAIR OF NINES (Solution)

North

♠ 5 4 3
♡ J 9 8 2
◇ J 7 4
♣ J 9 2

West

♠ 7 6
♡ K 6 5 4 3
◇ K Q 3 2
♣ 4 3

East

♠ 10 8
♡ A Q
◇ A 10 9 8 5
♣ K 8 7 6

South

♠ A K Q J 9 2
♡ 10 7
◇ 6
♣ A Q 10 5

You have two heart losers plus a diamond loser so you need to find East with the king of clubs to make the hand. He probably has it. West appears to have started with the K Q of diamonds (from the lead) placing most of the remaining high cards with East.

Furthermore, you have to reach dummy to take the club finesse. There is only one possible dummy entry and that is in the trump suit—if the opponents trumps divide 2-2, and, if you do not ruff with the precious DEUCE of spades at trick two!

You must ruff with the nine in the hopes that spades are 2-2. Once they are, don't relax, your problems are still not over. Take a good look at that club suit. If you lead the jack and East ducks, you will be forced to win the second club in your hand. When the suit divides 4-2 you wind up losing a trick to the king.

Now observe what happens if you begin with the NINE. East plays low and you underplay with the five. Now lead the jack underplaying the ten, remaining in dummy if East does not cover. You wind up with an easy four tricks.

KEY LESSON POINTERS

1. WITH A HUMONGOUS TRUMP HOLDING, IT IS ALMOST NEVER RIGHT TO RUFF WITH YOUR LOWEST TRUMP EARLY ON. THAT LOWEST TRUMP CAN SERVE MANY USEFUL PURPOSES—THE MOST LIKELY BEING A POSSIBLE LATER ENTRY TO DUMMY.
2. WHEN YOU HAVE AQ10x FACING J9x, OR AJ10x FACING Q9x START WITH THE NINE—NOT WITH THE HONOR.

(81) WHEN TRUMPS DON'T BREAK

East-West vulnerable
Dealer South

North
♠ 9 7 6 4
♡ Q 10 7 5
♢ K 9 3
♣ 5 4

South
♠ Q J 10 8
♡ A K J
♢ A Q 2
♣ K Q 3

South	West	North	East
2 NT	Pass	3 ♣*	Pass
3 ♠	Pass	4 ♠	All Pass

*Asking for a four card major.

Opening lead: ♡ 9

You win with the king and play the queen of spades to East's king. East returns the jack of clubs. You cover with the king, but West wins the ace and returns the deuce of clubs to the eight and queen.

At trick five you lead the jack of spades which holds, East discarding a small diamond. How do you continue?

WHEN TRUMPS DON'T BREAK (Solution)

North

♠ 9 7 6 4
♡ Q 10 7 5
◇ K 9 3
♣ 5 4

West

♠ A 5 3 2
♡ 9 2
◇ 10 6 4
♣ A 7 6 2

East

♠ K
♡ 8 6 4 3
◇ J 8 7 5
♣ J 10 9 8

South

♠ Q J 10 8
♡ A K J
◇ A Q 2
♣ K Q 3

As it is always safer to draw all of the opponents trumps if possible, you must ask yourself what can happen if you play a third round of trumps.

For one thing, West can win and play a fourth round. Will that hurt you? Count your tricks. If West plays back a fourth trump, you will have two spade tricks, four hearts, three diamonds and a club. Ten tricks. Clearly it is right to continue playing trumps. Why put this hand in this book?

Because many players panic when they run into a bad trump division and neglect to count tricks. For example, if South had decided to trump a club before playing a third round of trumps, he goes down! Now when West wins the spade ace (with no trump remaining in dummy) he plays a fourth club forcing South to ruff with his last trump.

West's last trump becomes the setting trick.

KEY LESSON POINTERS

1. IF YOU CAN AFFORD TO PLAY A TRUMP CONTRACT AT NOTRUMP (EVEN IF IT MEANS DRAWING ALL OF THE TRUMPS FROM BOTH YOUR HAND AND DUMMY) DO IT.
2. DO NOT TRUMP IN ONE HAND PREMATURELY IF THE HAND CAN BE PLAYED IN NOTRUMP. YOU MAY LOSE CONTROL LATER.
3. IF A SIDE SUIT LOSER CAN EITHER BE TRUMPED IN DUMMY OR DISCARDED UPON A WINNER FROM DUMMY, IT IS SAFER TO DISCARD IT AFTER DRAWING TRUMPS—IF POSSIBLE. HERE IT IS POSSIBLE.
4. DON'T PANIC WHEN YOU RUN INTO A BAD TRUMP BREAK. SHOW A LITTLE CHARACTER.

(82) WHICH WAY?

East-West vulnerable
Dealer South

North

♠ K 10 3 2
♡ J 4 2
♢ Q J 9 3
♣ 6 4

South

♠ A J 5 4
♡ Q 7 6
♢ A K 8 2
♣ A K

South	West	North	East
2 NT	Pass	3 ♣	Pass
3 ♠	Pass	4 ♠	All Pass

Opening lead: ♣ Q

East plays the deuce. Plan this play.

WHICH WAY? (Solution)

North

♠ K 10 3 2
♡ J 4 2
◇ Q J 9 3
♣ 6 4

West

♠ Q 9 8
♡ K 8 5 3
◇ 10 5
♣ Q J 10 3

East

♠ 7 6
♡ A 10 9
◇ 7 6 4
♣ 9 8 7 5 2

South

♠ A J 5 4
♡ Q 7 6
◇ A K 8 2
♣ A K

You should notice: (1) there are four possible losers, three hearts and a spade: (2) both you and your partner have the exact same distribution: (3) hearts is a suit you would prefer the opponents lead to you: (4) You are in yet another touchy contract.

Hands that have "mirrored" distributions lend themselves to throw-ins and end plays. This is no exception.

The idea is to force a heart lead. You have no minor suit losers but you do have a possible trump loser. Why not use the trump suit as your throw-in suit?

Play the ace-king of spades. If the queen drops, fine, you can no longer lose the hand. Simply draw the last trump, take your minor suit winners and lead a heart yourself. At worst you lose three heart tricks.

Assume the queen of spades has not fallen. Cash the second round of clubs and run the diamonds. If somebody ruffs, it will be with the queen of spades and that person will either have to lead a heart, eliminating one of your heart losers, or lead a club—a ruff and a sluff—with the same result.

If nobody ruffs a diamond, lead a spade. Whoever has the queen will be forced to attack hearts or give you a ruff and a sluff.

KEY LESSON POINTERS

1. A TRUMP LOSER CAN BE USED AS YOUR THROW-IN CARD AFTER THE SIDE SUITS HAVE BEEN STRIPPED.
2. WHEN STRIPPING, CASH SHORT SUITS BEFORE LONG SUITS TO AVOID AN EARLY RUFF FOLLOWED BY A SAFE EXIT. (CLUBS FIRST)

(83) NO SECOND CHOICE

Neither side vulnerable
Dealer South

North
♠ A Q 10 2
♡ Q 9 8 7
◇ A 2
♣ 6 4 3

South
♠ 8 6
♡ A K J 5 4 3
◇ 5 4
♣ Q J 10

South	West	North	East
1 ♡	Dbl.	Rdbl.	3 ◇*
Pass	Pass	4 ♡	All Pass

*Weak

Opening lead: ♣ K

East begins a high-low in clubs and West continues with the ace and deuce of clubs, East ruffing the third round. East switches to the Jack of diamonds. Plan the play.

NO SECOND CHOICE (Solution)

North
♠ A Q 10 2
♡ Q 9 8 7
◇ A 2
♣ 6 4 3

West
♠ K J 9 7
♡ 2
◇ Q 8 3
♣ A K 9 5 2

East
♠ 5 4 3
♡ 10 6
◇ K J 10 9 7 6
♣ 8 7

South
♠ 8 6
♡ A K J 5 4 3
◇ 5 4
♣ Q J 10

Things have taken a turn for the worse with East ruffing your club winner and shifting to a diamond. Time to take stock.

You have a diamond loser and a possible, but unlikely, spade loser on the bidding. West figures to have most of the missing high card strength.

The point is that you must get rid of that diamond loser somewhere and it has to go on the spades. You really have no choice. After drawing trumps you must finesse the TEN of spades, playing West for both missing honors. If your finesse works, simply reenter your hand and finesse the queen of spades to dispose of the losing diamond.

KEY LESSON POINTERS

1. WHEN YOUR LOSER COUNT TELLS YOU THAT YOU MUST PLAY A SIDE SUIT WITH MAXIMUM RISK, THEN PLAY THAT SUIT ACCORDINGLY.
2. JUMP BIDS DIRECTLY OVER STRENGTH SHOWING REDOUBLES ARE PREEMPTIVE.

(84) THE BEST GRAND

East-West vulnerable
Dealer South

North

♠ K 7 6
♡ K Q 7 5
♢ Q J 3 2
♣ A 3

South

♠ A Q 3 2
♡ A 3
♢ A K 6 4
♣ K 5 4

South	West	North	East
2 NT	Pass	3 ♣*	Pass
3 ♠	Pass	5 NT**	Pass
6 ♢	Pass	7 ♢!!***	All Pass

*Stayman (asking for a four card major)
**Asking for another four card suit.
***Going beserk.

Opening lead: ♣ Q

Plan the play.

THE BEST GRAND (Solution)

North
♠ K 7 6
♡ K Q 7 5
◇ Q J 3 2
♣ A 3

West
♠ J 9
♡ 10 8 6 4
◇ 5
♣ Q J 10 9 8 7

East
♠ 10 8 5 4
♡ J 9 2
◇ 10 9 8 7
♣ 6 2

South
♠ A Q 3 2
♡ A 3
◇ A K 6 4
♣ K 5 4

Counting tricks, which is a bit easier when playing slam contracts with a 4-4 trump fit, (both hands balanced) gives you: three spades, three hearts, four diamonds and two clubs for a grand total of twelve.

Win the ace of clubs and play the ace and a diamond to the queen. If diamonds divide 3-2 draw the last trump and claim. If West has the four diamonds, ruff a club in dummy. West plays before dummy and will not be able to hurt you if he happened to have started with a doubleton club. If East has the four diamonds, play ace of hearts, king of hearts, and ruff a low heart in your hand. Even if East is short in hearts he will not be able to hurt you because you play after East.

KEY LESSON POINTERS

1. WHEN PLAYING A 4-4 TRUMP FIT WITH BOTH HANDS BALANCED IT IS EASIER TO COUNT TRICKS THAN LOSERS.
2. IF ONE EXTRA TRICK BY RUFFING IS NEEDED, IT IS SAFER TO RUFF IN THE HAND THAT CANNOT BE OVERRUFFED. (PRESUMABLY YOU WILL KNOW WHICH OF THE TWO DEFENDING HANDS HAS THE REMAINING TRUMP(S).
3. IF THE RUFF CAN BE TAKEN IN EITHER HAND, THE TWO ROUNDS OF TRUMPS SHOULD BE DRAWN IN SUCH A FASHION AS TO LEAVE A HIGH AND A LOW TRUMP ON EACH SIDE.
4. IF MORE THAN ONE RUFF IS NEEDED, IT IS USUALLY RIGHT TO RUFF IN THE HAND THAT HAS THE WEAKER TRUMP HOLDING USING THE STRONGER TRUMP HOLDING TO DRAW THE OUTSTANDING TRUMPS.

(85) IT WORKS!

Neither side vulnerable
Dealer South

North

♠ 10 8
♡ 6 4 3
♢ 9 7 5 2
♣ 8 6 4 3

South

♠ A K Q J 5 3
♡ A Q J
♢ A 6 3
♣ 5

South	West	North	East
2 ♣*	Pass	2 ♢**	Pass
2 ♠	Pass	2 NT	Pass
4 ♠	All Pass		

*Strong and artificial
**Negative response

Opening lead: ♣ Q

The queen holds. West continues with the deuce of clubs to East's king. Plan the play.

IT WORKS! (Solution)

North

♠ 10 8
♡ 6 4 3
♢ 9 7 5 2
♣ 8 6 4 3

West

♠ 9 7 6
♡ 9 8 5
♢ K Q 4
♣ Q J 10 2

East

♠ 4 2
♡ K 10 7 2
♢ J 10 8
♣ A K 9 7

South

♠ A K Q J 5 3
♡ A Q J
♢ A 6 3
♣ 5

Again you must plan before you play! You have lost a club and you are doomed to lose two diamond tricks. In order to make this hand you must find the king of hearts with East. Furthermore, unless it is singleton or doubleton, (unlikely) you are going to have to take two finesses to pick it up!

This means you need TWO dummy entries. Do you have them? Only if you have the guts to ruff the second club high, finesse the eight of spades, take the heart finesse, back to the ten of spades to repeat the heart finesse. Congratulations.

KEY LESSON POINTERS

1. DO NOT PLAY HASTILY TO THE FIRST TRICK OR TWO. PLAN THE HAND IN ADVANCE.
2. IF YOU NEED A PARTICULAR CARD IN A PARTICULAR PLACE TO MAKE YOUR CONTRACT, ASSUME IT IS THERE. IF THAT IS STILL NOT ENOUGH, MAKE MORE POSITIVE ASSUMPTIONS.
3. BE CAREFUL ABOUT RUFFING WITH A LOW TRUMP EARLY ON WHEN YOU HAVE A STRONG TRUMP SUIT AND THE ONLY ENTRIES TO PARTNER'S HAND ARE IN THE TRUMP SUIT.

(86) THE FULL FAKE

Neither side vulnerable
Dealer West

North

- ♠ K 7 2
- ♡ K 10 8
- ♢ J 5 3
- ♣ Q J 6 2

South

- ♠ Q J 10 8 5 3
- ♡ A 7
- ♢ A 7 6
- ♣ K 7

West	North	East	South
1 ♢	Pass	Pass	2 ♠
Pass	4 ♠	All Pass	

Opening lead: ♢ K   East plays the eight.

Plan the play.

THE FULL FAKE (Solution)

North

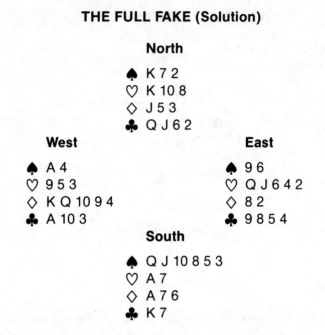

♠ K 7 2
♡ K 10 8
◇ J 5 3
♣ Q J 6 2

West

♠ A 4
♡ 9 5 3
◇ K Q 10 9 4
♣ A 10 3

East

♠ 9 6
♡ Q J 6 4 2
◇ 8 2
♣ 9 8 5 4

South

♠ Q J 10 8 5 3
♡ A 7
◇ A 7 6
♣ K 7

You have to lose a spade, a club, a diamond and almost certainly a diamond ruff judging from East's play at trick one.

Your best bet is to win the opening lead and try the JACK of spades at trick two. If West can be induced into thinking you are taking a spade finesse, he may play low. Once he ducks, East will be out of spades to ruff a third round of diamonds when you play a second trump. You are so tricky.

KEY LESSON POINTERS

1. WHEN IT IS IMPORTANT TO AVOID A RUFF, AND YOU ARE MISSING THE ACE OF TRUMPS, BY MAKING IT APPEAR YOU ARE TRYING TO TAKE A FINESSE IN THE TRUMP SUIT, THE PLAYER HOLDING THE ACE MAY DUCK ONE ROUND. THAT MAY BE ALL YOU NEED.
2. WHEN YOU WANT YOUR OPPONENTS TO DUCK A TRICK OR NOT COVER AN HONOR, LEAD A LOWER HONOR FROM YOUR EQUAL HONORS. WHEN YOU WANT THEM TO COVER OR TAKE THE TRICK, LEAD THE HIGHER OR HIGHEST HONOR.

(87) STAY AWAKE!

North-South vulnerable
Dealer East

North

♠ A 7 6
♡ K 9 5
◇ Q 10 7
♣ A 5 3 2

South

♠ Q J 10 9 8
♡ Q J 10 8
◇ J 5 2
♣ 9

East	South	West	North
Pass	Pass	Pass	1 ♣
Pass	1 ♠	Pass	1 NT
2 ♣*	2 ♡	3 ♣	3 ♠
All Pass			

*Natural

Opening lead: ◇ K

East signals with the eight and West continues with the ace of diamonds, East playing the six. West continues with the three of diamonds, East trumping with the deuce.

At trick four East shifts to the queen of clubs, West playing the seven. Plan the play.

STAY AWAKE! (Solution)

North
♠ A 7 6
♡ K 9 5
◇ Q 10 7
♣ A 5 3 2

West
♠ 5 4 3
♡ 7 6
◇ A K 9 4 3
♣ K 7 6

East
♠ K 2
♡ A 4 3 2
◇ 8 6
♣ Q J 10 9 4

South
♠ Q J 10 9 8
♡ Q J 10 8
◇ J 5 2
♣ 8

You have lost three tricks and you must lose a heart. The problem revolves around spades and, of course, the normal play is to finesse. However, there are extenuating circumstances here.

Both East and West have passed originally and West has turned up with a five card diamond suit headed by the AK. Furthermore, if East's return of the queen of clubs and West's signal with the seven are to be believed, West has the king of clubs. If West has the king of clubs along with the AK of diamonds, he simply can't have the king of spades and pass originally.

You might lead a heart to your hand in order to lead the queen of spades, but when West plays low rise with the ace—or, simply play the ace of spades, quoting the rabbi's rule, "when the king is singleton, play the ace".

KEY LESSON POINTERS

1. DON'T FORGET THE BIDDING. IT IS YOUR LIFELINE.
2. IF YOU CAN AFFORD THE LUXURY OF LEADING AN HONOR TOWARDS ANOTHER HONOR,—EVEN IF YOU HAVE NO INTENTION OF FINESS-ING—BY ALL MEANS DO SO. EVERY SO OFTEN YOU WILL HAVE MIS-CALCULATED, BUT A FRIENDLY OPPONENT MAY COME TO YOUR RESCUE BY COVERING. FOR EXAMPLE, WITH KJ10 9 FACING Axxx IN DUMMY, IT IS A SIN TO LEAD THE NINE OR TEN TO THE ACE WITH THE INTENTION OF FINESSING ON THE WAY BACK. LEAD THE JACK. YOU MAY NOT HAVE TO FINESSE ANYTHING. A FRIEND, RELATIVE, OR DODO MAY COVER.

(88) SQUANDER NOT

Both sides vulnerable
Dealer North

North
- ♠ 8 4
- ♡ A Q 9 8 7
- ♢ K 6 5
- ♣ 8 4 3

South
- ♠ A
- ♡ K J 10 6 5
- ♢ A J
- ♣ A J 10 5 2

North	East	South	West
Pass	Pass	1 ♡	1 ♠
3 ♡	4 ♠	6 ♡	All Pass

Opening lead: ♠ Q

With whom do they think they are kidding around? Now all you have to do is make it. Can you see what your best play is? Trumps are 2-1.

SQUANDER NOT (Solution)

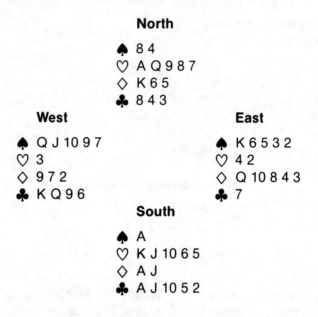

North
- ♠ 8 4
- ♡ A Q 9 8 7
- ◇ K 6 5
- ♣ 8 4 3

West
- ♠ Q J 10 9 7
- ♡ 3
- ◇ 9 7 2
- ♣ K Q 9 6

East
- ♠ K 6 5 3 2
- ♡ 4 2
- ◇ Q 10 8 4 3
- ♣ 7

South
- ♠ A
- ♡ K J 10 6 5
- ◇ A J
- ♣ A J 10 5 2

This is another recognition problem. Losers in only one suit—clubs—, a strong trump holding on both sides, and two other suits that can be eliminated before clubs are attacked.

Nevertheless there is a bit of planning to do here. You must end up in dummy when leading a club and you must remain with trumps on both sides.

Cross to a trump at trick two and ruff a spade, next play ace-king and ruff a diamond and then draw the last trump ending in dummy. If you draw the second trump before you ruff the diamond you will find yourself short a trump and you will be unable to execute the strip.

Once the hand is stripped, the hand is over. Lead a club. If East follows with a low club, insert the ten or jack and claim. West, upon winning the club will be hopelessly endplayed.

KEY LESSON POINTERS

1. WHEN PLANNING A STRIP AND END PLAY THAT REQUIRES YOU TO END UP IN ONE PARTICULAR HAND, BE SURE YOU HAVE THE ENTRIES TO DO JUST THAT. THIS COULD MEAN NOT DRAWING TRUMPS IMMEDIATELY, RATHER USING THE TRUMP SUIT AS THE COMMUNICATION SUIT.
2. IF THERE IS A SHORTAGE OF ENTRIES AND/OR THE HAND CANNOT BE CONVENIENTLY STRIPPED, DO NOT KNOCK YOURSELF OUT TRYING THE IMPOSSIBLE. LOOK AROUND FOR SOMETHING ELSE.

(89)   QUESTIONS, QUESTIONS

Neither side vulnerable
Dealer North

North
- ♠ K 6
- ♡ A 3 2
- ♢ A Q 5 4 2
- ♣ J 5 2

South
- ♠ A Q J 10 9 8
- ♡ K J 5
- ♢ 9 3
- ♣ 4 3

North	East	South	West
1 ♢	Pass	1 ♠	Pass
1 NT	Pass	4 ♠	All Pass

Opening lead: ♣ K

West continues with the ace and a club to East's queen which you ruff. You lead a diamond to the queen and king. East returns the four of hearts. Question time.

Before you took the diamond finesse, how many losers did you have, how many tricks?

Why did you finesse diamonds before drawing trumps?

Why did you finesse diamonds before hearts?

Which heart do you play at this point?

What is your general plan?

Are you sick of all these questions?

QUESTIONS, QUESTIONS (Solution)

North

♠ K 6
♡ A 3 2
◇ A Q 5 4 2
♣ J 5 2

West

♠ 7 2
♡ Q 9 8
◇ 10 8 7 6
♣ A K 10 7

East

♠ 5 4 3
♡ 10 7 6 4
◇ K J
♣ Q 9 8 6

South

♠ A Q J 10 9 8
♡ K J 5
◇ 9 3
♣ 4 3

After ruffing the third round of clubs, you had two possible losers, one in diamonds and one in hearts. Your trick count was nine—six spades, two hearts plus one diamond. It never hurts to check both tricks and losers.

You finesse diamonds before drawing trumps because you may need the king of spades as a helping entry to establish the diamonds in case of a 4-2 diamond break.

You finessed diamonds before hearts because diamonds is the LONG suit. Finesses in short suits come LAST.

You should play the KING of hearts when East returns a heart to preserve the ace as a future entry to the diamond suit—now continue establishing the diamonds to get rid of the losing heart.

After winning the king of hearts, play the ace and ruff a diamond. If diamonds break 3-3 (they only do for your opponents) draw trumps and enter dummy with the ace of hearts to discard the losing heart on the good diamond(s).

If diamonds break 4-2, enter dummy with the KING OF SPADES and ruff another diamond. Now draw trumps and use the remaining diamond to pitch the heart loser. The FINAL entry being the ace of hearts.

KEY LESSON POINTERS

1. COUNT LOSERS AS WELL AS SURE TRICKS BEFORE PLANNING THE PLAY.

2. WHEN ESTABLISHING A SIDE SUIT THAT HAS OUTSIDE ENTRIES IN BOTH THE TRUMP SUIT AND SIDE SUIT, USE THE TRUMP ENTRIES FIRST. IF YOU DO IT VICE VERSA, YOU WILL HAVE TO DRAW TRUMPS ENDING IN DUMMY. THAT MAY NOT BE POSSIBLE.

(90)   BACK AND FORTH

Neither side vulnerable
Dealer North

North

♠ K Q 9 8
♡ A 9 8 7 5
♢ 3
♣ A K Q

South

♠ A J 10 7
♡ 4
♢ A 9 8 7 4
♣ 4 3 2

North	East	South	West
1 ♡	Pass	1 ♠	Pass
4 ♢*	Pass	6 ♠	All Pass

*Singleton diamond with four card spade support.

Opening lead: ♣ J

East follows. Plan the play.

BACK AND FORTH (Solution)

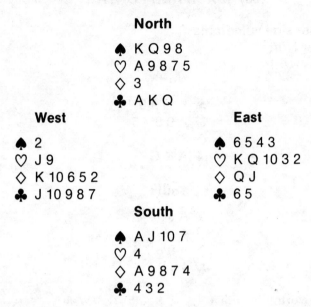

North
- ♠ K Q 9 8
- ♡ A 9 8 7 5
- ◇ 3
- ♣ A K Q

West
- ♠ 2
- ♡ J 9
- ◇ K 10 6 5 2
- ♣ J 10 9 8 7

East
- ♠ 6 5 4 3
- ♡ K Q 10 3 2
- ◇ Q J
- ♣ 6 5

South
- ♠ A J 10 7
- ♡ 4
- ◇ A 9 8 7 4
- ♣ 4 3 2

Blessed with high trumps as well as a singleton on both sides, you should consider a crossruff.

In the suits that you will be crossruffing, hearts and diamonds you have a total of ten tricks; the two red aces as well as eight trump tricks—four on each side.

What this means is that you need TWO, not three additional side suit tricks. Therefore you should cash TWO club tricks BEFORE embarking upon your crossruff. With a trump lead, limiting you to seven trump tricks, you would have to try to cash three club tricks before crossruffing.

KEY LESSON POINTERS

1. WHEN CONSIDERING A CROSSRUFF FIRST COUNT YOUR TRICKS IN THE SUITS YOU ARE PLANNING TO CROSSRUFF. THIS COUNT SHOULD INCLUDE HIGH CARD TRICKS IN THE TWO SUITS YOU ARE RUFFING, (IN THIS CASE TWO RED ACES) PLUS THE NUMBER OF TRUMP TRICKS YOU WILL OBTAIN.

2. ONCE YOU HAVE COUNTED YOUR SIDE SUIT WINNERS PLUS TRUMP TRICKS IN THE SUITS YOU ARE CROSSRUFFING, YOU WILL KNOW HOW MANY TRICKS YOU NEED TO CASH IN THE REMAINING SUIT BEFORE BEGINNING YOUR CROSSRUFF.

3. NO NEED TO TRY TO CASH MORE TRICKS THAN NECESSARY BEFORE YOU BEGIN YOUR CROSSRUFF. SOMEONE MAY RUFF AND RETURN A TRUMP. THIS BIT OF CARELESSNESS (GREED?) WILL INEVITABLY RESULT IN A POSTMORTEM LECTURE ON HOW TO PLAY A CROSS-RUFF. FOREWARNED. . . . .

(91)   MORE DANGER!

North-South vulnerable
Dealer South

North

♠ A J 10 9
♡ 8 6 2
♢ 8 7
♣ K 10 9 3

South

♠ Q 5 3
♡ K Q 9
♢ A K 10
♣ A Q J 4

South	West	North	East
2 NT	Pass	3 ♣*	Pass
3 ♢**	Pass	3 NT	All Pass

*Artificial—asking for a four card major.
**No four card major.

Opening lead: ♡ 5

East plays the jack. Should you take this trick? What is your plan?

MORE DANGER! (Solution)

North
♠ A J 10 9
♡ 8 6 2
♢ 8 7
♣ K 10 9 3

West
♠ 6 4 2
♡ A 10 7 5 3
♢ J 9 5
♣ 7 6

East
♠ K 8 7
♡ J 4
♢ Q 6 4 3 2
♣ 8 5 2

South
♠ Q 5 3
♡ K Q 9
♢ A K 10
♣ A Q J 4

First things first. Count tricks! You have four clubs, two diamonds, one heart and one spade. East's play of the jack of hearts places West with the A 10. East is the danger hand because he can lead through your honor combination in hearts if you win the trick.

As you are going to have to develop your extra trick(s) in spades, you should duck the opening lead—ye olde hold-up play. This ducking play protects you against a doubleton heart along with the king of spades in the East hand.

Assume you duck the opening lead. East continues a heart (say) and the best West can do is win his ace. He is now helpless. You win any return and run the queen of spades and claim the balance after it loses.

KEY LESSON POINTERS

1. WHEN HOLDING A KING-QUEEN COMBINATION WITH THE FIRST FINESSE HEADED TO YOUR RIGHT—HOLD UP HOPING YOUR RIGHT OPPONENT HAS A DOUBLETON.

2. WHEN HOLDING A KING-QUEEN COMBINATION AND MISSING A SIDE ACE, WIN THE FIRST TRICK IF YOU THINK THE ACE IS TO YOUR LEFT, HOLD UP IF YOU THINK IT IS TO YOUR RIGHT. IF YOU HAVE NO IDEA, KEEP IN MIND THAT IF LEFT HAND OPPONENT DID NOT BID HE IS UNLIKELY TO HAVE BOTH ACES. BETTER TO PLAY FOR SPLIT ACES AND HOLD UP.

3. IN ALL CASES, COUNT YOUR SURE TRICKS FIRST TO SEE WHETHER IT IS EVEN NECESSARY TO HOLD UP AND/OR IF THERE IS A RISK OF A SHIFT TO A WEAKER SUIT.

(92) ALL BUT ONE

North-South vulnerable
Dealer South

North
♠ 9 4 3
♡ A K 9 7
◇ A K Q J
♣ 10 9

South
♠ K Q
♡ 6 4 3
◇ 5 4 3 2
♣ A K Q J

South	West	North	East
1 NT	Pass	2 ♣*	Pass
2 ◇	Pass	6 NT	All Pass

*Asking for a four card major

Opening lead: ♠ J

After the hand you will show your partner how he should have managed to arrive at the superior contract of six diamonds. For the time being you will concentrate on making six notrump.

East wins the ace of spades and returns the deuce of spades. Plan the play.

ALL BUT ONE (Solution)

North

♠ 9 4 3
♡ A K 9 7
◇ A K Q J
♣ 10 9

West

♠ J 10 8 7
♡ J 8 5 2
◇ 10 6
♣ 8 4 2

East

♠ A 6 5 2
♡ Q 10
◇ 9 8 7
♣ 7 6 5 3

South

♠ K Q
♡ 6 4 3
◇ 5 4 3 2
♣ A K Q J

You have eleven top tricks with only one chance for a twelfth—a squeeze. Your threat suits are spades (the nine) and hearts. Both threats are in the same hand and only one suit (hearts) has an entry.

Proper squeeze technique calls for playing the non-threat suits first (diamonds and clubs) ending up in the hand OPPOSITE the entry. The entry is in the North hand, so play diamonds and then clubs ending in South.

West, who controls both spades and hearts will be unable to guard both suits on the play of the last club. Presto, a squeeze!

KEY LESSON POINTERS

1. HANDS THAT HAVE ALL THE TRICKS BUT ONE ARE CANDIDATES FOR A SQUEEZE IF THERE ARE AT LEAST TWO THREAT SUITS.
2. A THREAT SUIT IS ANY SUIT WHICH HAS THE POSSIBILITY OF SCORING AN EXTRA TRICK IF THE OPPONENTS EITHER DISCARD A KEY CARD IN THE SUIT, OR DISCARD ENOUGH CARDS IN THE SUIT TO MAKE YOUR SMALLER CARDS WINNERS.
3. IN ORDER TO PULL OFF A SQUEEZE AT LEAST ONE OF THE THREAT SUITS MUST HAVE AN ENTRY TO IT.
4. THE NON-THREAT SUITS ARE PLAYED FIRST.
5. WHEN ONLY ONE THREAT SUIT HAS AN ENTRY (HEARTS), DECLARER MUST CASH HIS NON-THREAT SUIT WINNERS WINDING UP IN THE HAND OPPOSITE THAT ENTRY.
6. IF BOTH THREAT SUITS ARE IN THE SAME HAND, (THE WORST) ONLY THE OPPONENT THAT SITS IN FRONT OF THE THREAT SUITS CAN BE SQUEEZED.

(93) PRETTY HIGH

East-West vulnerable
Dealer South

North

♠ J 10 6
♡ A 4 2
◇ A K J 10 4
♣ A 5

South

♠ A K Q
♡ Q J 10
◇ 3 2
♣ K Q J 10 9

South	West	North	East
1 ♣	Pass	1 ◇	Pass
2 NT	Pass	7 NT	All Pass

Opening lead: ♠ 9

Obviously, you are playing with someone who doesn't kid around. What is your best play to land this grand?

PRETTY HIGH (Solution)

North
♠ J 10 6
♡ A 4 2
◇ A K J 10 4
♣ A 5

West

♠ 9 8 7 2
♡ 8 3
◇ 9 8 6 5
♣ 8 3 2

East

♠ 5 4 3
♡ K 9 7 6 5
◇ Q 7
♣ 7 6 4

South
♠ A K Q
♡ Q J 10
◇ 3 2
♣ K Q J 10 9

You have eleven top tricks and can make the hand if either red suit finesse works. Which one should you take?

COMBINE your chances by playing the ace-king of diamonds. If the queen has not dropped, take the heart finesse.

Incidentally if a heart had been led, psychological factors come into play. It is HIGHLY unlikely that anyone would underlead a king into the jaws of a two notrump rebidder in a contract of seven notrump. Therefore, with a heart lead rise with the ace and take a first round diamond finesse.

KEY LESSON POINTERS

1. WHEN PLAYING A CONTRACT THAT CAN BE MADE IF EITHER ONE OF TWO FINESSES SUCCEED, BUT YOU CAN ONLY TAKE ONE SAFELY, PLAY THE ACE-KING OF THE LONGER SUIT AND IF THE QUEEN HAS NOT DROPPED TAKE A FINESSE IN THE SHORTER SUIT.

2. IF THERE HAS BEEN NO INDICATION OF A LONG SUIT IN EITHER DUMMY OR DECLARER'S HAND, MOST PLAYERS MAKE PASSIVE LEADS AGAINST CONTRACTS OF SIX OR SEVEN NOTRUMP.

(94) COUNT!

Neither side vulnerable
Dealer East

North
♠ 6 5 4 3
♡ J 9 4
♢ Q 9 8
♣ A K 9

South
♠ A K 10 9 8 7
♡ 3 2
♢ K 10 5
♣ 3 2

East	South	West	North
1 NT*	2 ♠	Pass	3 ♠
Pass	4 ♠	All Pass	

*16–18

Opening lead: ♡ 5

East plays the queen of hearts and continues with the king and ace of hearts which you ruff. West following with the six and seven.

You play the ace-king of spades and East follows with the jack and queen. West discarding a small club on the second spade. Postponing the inevitable, you play the ace-king and ruff a club East following low, and then playing the jack and queen. How do you play the diamond suit?

COUNT! (Solution)

North

♠ 6 5 4 3
♡ J 9 4
◇ Q 9 8
♣ A K 9

West

♠ 2
♡ 10 7 6 5
◇ A 7 3
♣ 10 8 7 5 4

East

♠ Q J
♡ A K Q 8
◇ J 6 4 2
♣ Q J 6

South

♠ A K 10 9 8 7
♡ 3 2
◇ K 10 5
♣ 3 2

East has turned up with three points in spades, nine in hearts and three in clubs for a grand total of 15. He cannot have the ace of diamonds as that would give him 19 and he needs the jack of diamonds to get up to 16.

Play a diamond to the queen and finesse the ten on the way back.

KEY LESSON POINTERS

1. NOTICE YOUR OPPONENTS' NOTRUMP RANGES. IT CERTAINLY HELPS IN THE PLAY, ALTHOUGH YOU SHOULDN'T COUNT ON PLAYING TOO MANY HANDS WHEN AN OPPONENT OPENS A STRONG NOTRUMP.
2. WHEN YOU DISCOVER DURING THE PLAY THAT AN OPPONENT WHO HAS OPENED THE BIDDING WITH ONE OF A SUIT HAS A BALANCED HAND, THERE MUST BE A REASON WHY HE DID NOT OPEN ONE NOTRUMP. THE REASON PROBABLY IS THAT HE WAS EITHER TOO WEAK OR TOO STRONG. USE THIS INFORMATION TO HELP YOU DURING THE PLAY.

(95) IT WILL STILL BE THERE

North-South vulnerable
Dealer South

North
♠ 7
♡ K Q J 4
◇ 10 8 7 3 2
♣ A Q 5

South
♠ A 10
♡ 2
◇ A K J 9 6 5
♣ 7 4 3 2

South	West	North	East
1 ◇	Pass	1 ♡	1 ♠
2 ◇	3 ♠*	5 ◇	All Pass

*Preemptive

Opening lead: ♣ J

What is your plan?

IT WILL STILL BE THERE (Solution)

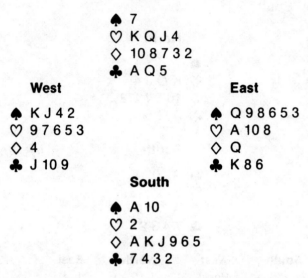

North

♠ 7
♡ K Q J 4
◇ 10 8 7 3 2
♣ A Q 5

West

♠ K J 4 2
♡ 9 7 6 5 3
◇ 4
♣ J 10 9

East

♠ Q 9 8 6 5 3
♡ A 10 8
◇ Q
♣ K 8 6

South

♠ A 10
♡ 2
◇ A K J 9 6 5
♣ 7 4 3 2

The have found your weak spot, the rats. You would like to set up your hearts for clubs discards, but now it seems as if you won't have TIME.

Don't panic. Count your losers and act as if nothing terrible has happened. You have two possible club losers and one heart loser.

Notice the effect of the play of the ACE of clubs at trick one. It still leaves the queen in dummy. If East has the ace of hearts, (likely) you will be able to knock out the ace of hearts while maintaining a club stopper.

Your play should be, ace of clubs, draw trumps, lead a heart. If East has the ace you are home free. If West has the ace of hearts, wins the first lead, and returns a club, you can always hope that East has a doubleton king.

KEY LESSON POINTERS

1. WITH AQx IN DUMMY FACING SMALL CARDS IN YOUR HAND, IT IS FREQUENTLY ADVISABLE TO GO UP WITH THE ACE WHEN THE SUIT IS LED. IN THAT WAY YOU STILL HAVE A STOPPER WHENEVER YOUR RIGHT HAND OPPONENT GETS THE LEAD. ALSO, IF THE OPENING LEADER ACTUALLY HAS THE KING YOU WILL MAKE YOUR QUEEN LATER. OF COURSE, IF YOU CANNOT AFFORD TO LOSE ANY TRICKS IN THE SUIT, YOU MUST TAKE A FIRST ROUND FINESSE.

2. WHEN IT COMES TO UNDERLEADING A KING, YOU MUST: (1) KNOW YOUR OPPONENTS—SOME ARE PSYCHOLOGICALLY INCAPABLE OF DOING IT: (2) BE FAMILIAR WITH THEIR LEAD CONVENTIONS. THE LEAD OF THE JACK MAY DENY A HIGHER HONOR. THIS TELLS YOU WHO HAS THE KING.

(96)   WRONG LEAD

East-West vulnerable
Dealer North

North
♠ A Q J 7 6
♡ J 9 3
◇ 4
♣ K Q 8 7

South
♠ 10 5
♡ K
◇ A K Q
♣ A J 10 6 5 4 3

North	East	South	West
1 ♠	Pass	2 ♣	Pass
3 ♣	Pass	4 NT	Pass
5 ◇	Pass	6 ♣	All Pass

Opening lead: ◇ J

What is your plan?

WRONG LEAD (Solution)

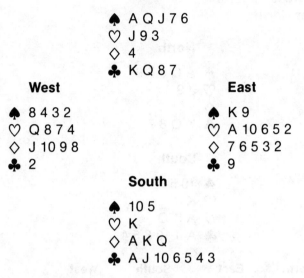

North
- ♠ A Q J 7 6
- ♡ J 9 3
- ◇ 4
- ♣ K Q 8 7

West
- ♠ 8 4 3 2
- ♡ Q 8 7 4
- ◇ J 10 9 8
- ♣ 2

East
- ♠ K 9
- ♡ A 10 6 5 2
- ◇ 7 6 5 3 2
- ♣ 9

South
- ♠ 10 5
- ♡ K
- ◇ A K Q
- ♣ A J 10 6 5 4 3

You have a heart loser and a possible spade loser. No finesse has worked in this book so far, so you really don't think this one will, do you?

One possibility is to enter dummy with a trump and either lead a low heart or the jack trying to sneak a heart before taking the spade finesse. That might be the winning play on some hands, but not this one.

You have a pretty good play available. Draw trump and cash your remaining two diamond winners discarding HEARTS from the table. Now that hearts have been evened off—one on each side—exit with a heart.

If East has the ace of hearts he is endplayed and you will not have to take the spade finesse. If West has the ace of hearts you will have to take that ¢&%*$ spade finesse after all.

KEY LESSON POINTERS

1. DECEPTIVELY, IT OFTEN WORKS TO LEAD A JACK FROM THE DUMMY TOWARDS A BARE KING. HOWEVER, IF SECOND HAND HOLDS BOTH THE ACE AND THE TEN, HE SHOULD REALIZE THAT SOMETHING FISHY MAY BE GOING ON.
2. WITH A SURE LOSER IN ONE SUIT AND A POSSIBLE FINESSE LOSER IN ANOTHER, IF YOU CAN POSSIBLY USE THE SUIT WITH THE SURE LOSER AS YOUR THROW-IN SUIT AFTER TRUMPS HAVE BEEN RE-MOVED AND THE OTHER SUIT STRIPPED—DO IT. ONE CAUTION. THE THROW-IN SUIT SHOULD BE EQUALLY DIVIDED BETWEEN YOUR HAND AND DUMMY TO PREVENT A SAFE EXIT IN THAT SUIT.
3. IN REAL LIFE FINESSES OCCASIONALLY WORK. NOT HERE!

(97)   TWO SINGLETONS

North-South vulnerable
Dealer South

North

♠ K Q 5
♡ J 3 2
◇ K Q
♣ A 10 9 8 2

South

♠ A J 10 9 8
♡ 7 6 5
◇ A J
♣ K 4 3

South	West	North	East
1 ♠	Pass	2 ♣	2 ♡
2 ♠	Pass	4 ♠	All Pass

Opening lead: ♡ 4

East wins the first three heart tricks, West shedding two diamonds. East shifts to a diamond which you win in dummy. You now play four rounds of spades, East following to all four, West discarding three more diamonds.

How do you continue from here?

TWO SINGLETONS (Solution)

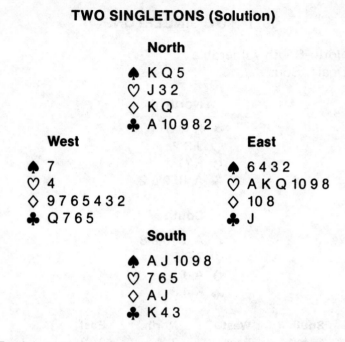

North

- ♠ K Q 5
- ♡ J 3 2
- ◇ K Q
- ♣ A 10 9 8 2

West

- ♠ 7
- ♡ 4
- ◇ 9 7 6 5 4 3 2
- ♣ Q 7 6 5

East

- ♠ 6 4 3 2
- ♡ A K Q 10 9 8
- ◇ 10 8
- ♣ J

South

- ♠ A J 10 9 8
- ♡ 7 6 5
- ◇ A J
- ♣ K 4 3

East is known to have six hearts, four spades and at least one diamond. In order to know how to tackle those clubs you must find out whether or not East has another diamond.

Play a second diamond. If East follows he can have at most one club. If that club is an honor you are home. Lead the king of clubs and finesse the ten if East plays an honor.

If East shows out on the second round of diamonds it means that he started with two clubs. Your only chance now is that those two clubs are the QJ doubleton.

KEY LESSON POINTERS

1. GET EVERY BIT OF INFORMATION YOU POSSIBLY CAN BEFORE ATTACKING A SUIT THAT OFFERS A VARIETY OF PLAYS.
2. KEEP TRACK OF ONLY ONE HAND—THE HAND THAT FIRST SHOWS UP WITH A LONG SUIT. FOR EXAMPLE, ON THIS HAND, YOU KNOW THAT EAST STARTED WITH SIX HEARTS THE MOMENT WEST DISCARDS ON THE SECOND ROUND OF HEARTS.
3. IT IS A BRIDGE SIN NOT TO KNOW HOW A SUIT WAS DIVIDED ORIGINALLY WHEN ONE PLAYER SHOWS OUT!

(98)　THE TEST

East-West vulnerable
Dealer East

North

♠ J 9 8
♡ A 10 8 6
◇ 10 7 5
♣ K J 9

South

♠ A K Q 10 7
♡ J 9 5
◇ Q 3
♣ A Q 10

East	South	West	North
1 ◇	Dbl.	Pass	2 ♡
Pass	2 ♠	Pass	3 ♠
Pass	4 ♠	All Pass	

Opening lead: ◇ 2

East wins the king and ace of diamonds and returns a third diamond which you ruff high, West playing the jack. You play the queen and ten of spades, both opponents following. How do you continue?

THE TEST (Solution)

North

♠ J 9 8
♡ A 10 8 6
◇ 10 7 5
♣ K J 9

West

♠ 6 3 2
♡ 4 3 2
◇ J 6 2
♣ 8 7 6 5

East

♠ 5 4
♡ K Q 7
◇ A K 9 8 4
♣ 4 3 2

South

♠ A K Q 10 7
♡ J 9 5
◇ Q 3
♣ A Q 10

Your only losers are in hearts and the normal play is to take two finesses. However you have some bidding to deal with. East has opened first seat, vulnerable, and has shown up with 7 high card points in diamonds. He cannot possibly have any honors in the black suits (you have them all) so he must have both heart honors and the "normal" play is doomed.

Better to play for a partial strip. Don't draw the last trump, cash three rounds of clubs ending in your hand and run the nine of hearts.

Assuming this loses to one of East's honors, with what can he exit safely if he doesn't have the missing trump? He can't.

If he returns a heart your troubles are over and if he returns a diamond (or a club if he has one) you ruff in dummy and discard a heart from your hand. Now cash the ace of hearts and the rest of your hand has nothing but high trumps. I just know you will be able to work it out from there.

KEY LESSON POINTERS

1. WHEN A PLAYER OPENS THE BIDDING FIRST SEAT (OR SECOND SEAT) HE SHOULD HAVE A MINIMUM OF 11 OR 12 HIGH CARD POINTS. PLAY THE HAND ACCORDINGLY.
2. REMEMBER, TO FORCE A LEAD IN A SUIT YOU WANT LED YOU MUST STRIP THE HAND THAT WILL WIN THE TRICK OF ALL SAFE EXITS. OCCASIONALLY THIS MEANS LEAVING A TRUMP AT LARGE SO THAT YOU CAN KEEP A TRUMP IN DUMMY TO HANDLE A RUFF AND A SLUFF. THE HAND THAT WINS THE TRICK MAY NOT HAVE THE ODD TRUMP AND WILL BE FORCED TO MAKE A TRICK LOSING LEAD.

(99) LONG SUITS

Neither side vulnerable
Dealer East

North

♠ 6 5
♡ K J 10
♢ Q J 10 9
♣ A 6 4 3

South

♠ K Q
♡ A 9 8 7 6 3
♢ 7 6 4
♣ K 7

East	South	West	North
Pass	1 ♡	3 ♠	4 ♡
All Pass			

Opening lead: ♠ A

West continues with the jack of spades, East playing nine-eight. You lead a low heart to the king, both following, and then the jack of hearts, East playing low. Do you finesse or not?

LONG SUITS (Solution)

North
♠ 6 5
♡ K J 10
◇ Q J 10 9
♣ A 6 4 3

West
♠ A J 10 7 4 3 2
♡ 2
◇ K 8 5
♣ 10 9

East
♠ 9 8
♡ Q 5 4
◇ A 4 3
♣ Q J 8 5 2

South
♠ K Q
♡ A 9 8 7 6 3
◇ 7 6 4
♣ K 7

Of course you should finesse. Can't you see that it works? Just kidding. The way to determine whether or not to finesse with nine cards between the two hands depends upon other DISTRIBUTIONAL INFORMATION.

For example, on this hand you KNOW that West started with seven spades and at least one heart for a total of eight cards. That means West has FIVE unknown cards. Consider East. You KNOW that East started with two spades and at least two hearts for a total of four cards. That means that East has NINE unknown cards.

The odds in favor of the finesse are 9-5.

KEY LESSON POINTERS

1. WHEN YOU HAVE NO INFORMATION TO GO BY, AND NO REASON TO FEAR FINESSING INTO ONE HAND OR THE OTHER, WITH NINE CARDS MISSING THE QUEEN, IT IS SLIGHTLY BETTER TO PLAY FOR THE DROP THAN TO TAKE A FINESSE.
2. HOWEVER, WHEN YOU KNOW THE ENTIRE DISTRIBUTION OF AN-OTHER SUIT(S), AS WELL AS THE INCONSEQUENTIAL CARDS IN THE CRITICAL SUIT, (IN THIS HAND, HEARTS) YOU SHOULD APPLY THE RULE OF VACANT SPACES.
3. WITHOUT GETTING TOO INVOLVED, SUBTRACT THE NUMBER OF CARDS BOTH PLAYERS ARE KNOWN TO HOLD (FROM THE BIDDING OR PLAY) FROM 13 TO DETERMINE HOW MANY VACANT SPACES EACH HAS. WHICHEVER PLAYER HAS MORE VACANT SPACES SHOULD BE PLAYED FOR THE MISSING CARD.

(100) AN OMINOUS SHIFT

East-West vulnerable
Dealer South

North
♠ A 2
♡ J 8 7
◇ K Q 10 7 6
♣ 6 5 3

South
♠ Q J 10 9 8 7
♡ A K
◇ A J 3
♣ 10 7

South	West	North	East
1 ♠	Pass	2 ◇	Pass
3 ♠	Pass	4 ♠	All Pass

Opening lead: ♣ K

East overtakes and shifts to the deuce of diamonds, an apparent singleton. Can you see any way out of this? Plan the play.

AN OMINOUS SHIFT (Solution)

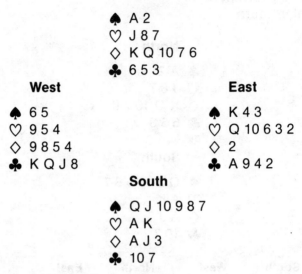

North
- ♠ A 2
- ♡ J 8 7
- ◇ K Q 10 7 6
- ♣ 6 5 3

West
- ♠ 6 5
- ♡ 9 5 4
- ◇ 9 8 5 4
- ♣ K Q J 8

East
- ♠ K 4 3
- ♡ Q 10 6 3 2
- ◇ 2
- ♣ A 9 4 2

South
- ♠ Q J 10 9 8 7
- ♡ A K
- ◇ A J 3
- ♣ 10 7

Unless East is the trickiest defender alive, he probably has the king of trumps and is planning to return a club upon getting in with the king of spades to secure a diamond ruff.

As you can see, if you play ace and a spade, East will do exactly that and the defense will enjoy four tricks—the king of spades, a diamond ruff and two clubs. What to do?

What you must do is stop East from putting West in with a club. How? Play the ace-king of hearts, enter dummy with the ace of spades (leading the queen) and play the jack of hearts. If East has the queen of hearts he will certainly play it, upon which you deposit your losing club. Now East has no way to get to the West hand and you make your contract.

KEY LESSON POINTERS

1. WHEN FACED WITH THE THREAT OF AN ADVERSE RUFF IT IS NOT ALWAYS RIGHT TO BEGIN DRAWING TRUMPS IMMEDIATELY, PARTICULARLY IF YOU HAVE A TRUMP LOSER.
2. CUTTING THE COMMUNICATIONS BETWEEN THE DEFENDER'S HANDS SOMETIMES TAKES PRIORITY OVER DRAWING TRUMPS.
3. WHEN TRYING TO AVOID A RUFF, THE DEFENDER WHO CAN GIVE HIS PARTNER THE RUFF IS THE DANGER HAND. IF YOU CAN SOMEHOW CUT COMMUNICATIONS TO THE DANGER HAND, YOU MAY BE ABLE TO AVOID THE RUFF.

(101) KEY CARD VICTORY

East-West vulnerable
Dealer North

North
♠ Q 3 2
♡ A 10 6 5
◇ K Q 3
♣ A J 2

South
♠ A K J 10 9
♡ 2
◇ A 7 6 4
♣ K Q 3

North	East	South	West
1 NT	Pass	3 ♠	Pass
4 ♠	Pass	4 NT*	Pass
5 ♠**	Pass	6 ◇***	Pass
7 ◇****	Pass	7 ♠	All Pass

*Roman Key Card Blackwood
**Two key cards plus the queen of trumps.
***What do you have in diamonds?
****The king and queen.

Opening lead: ♣ 10

Now that you have located the queen of trumps and the king-queen of diamonds by means of your lovely convention, for God's sake, don't blow the play. What is your plan?

KEY CARD VICTORY (Solution)

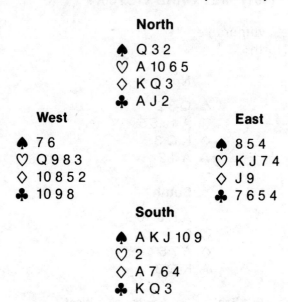

North

- ♠ Q 3 2
- ♡ A 10 6 5
- ◇ K Q 3
- ♣ A J 2

West

- ♠ 7 6
- ♡ Q 9 8 3
- ◇ 10 8 5 2
- ♣ 10 9 8

East

- ♠ 8 5 4
- ♡ K J 7 4
- ◇ J 9
- ♣ 7 6 5 4

South

- ♠ A K J 10 9
- ♡ 2
- ◇ A 7 6 4
- ♣ K Q 3

You have twelve tricks and, of course, one possible loser, the fourth diamond.

The best play by far is to win the club in your hand and play the ace-jack of spades. If spades break 4-1, you should try to trump your fourth diamond with dummy's queen of spades. You will have to be lucky for this to work. You will need the player with the four spades to also have four diamonds.

However, with a 3-2 spade division, things are looking up. Play the ace of hearts and ruff a heart, cross to dummy with a diamond and ruff another heart. Back to dummy with a low club to the jack and ruff dummy's last heart with your last trump. Now reenter dummy with a diamond and discard your diamond loser on dummy's queen of trumps.

KEY LESSON POINTERS

1. BY RUFFING THREE TIMES IN THE LONG HAND WHEN PLAYING A 5-3 TRUMP FIT YOU WILL BE ABLE TO DISCARD A LOSER ON DUMMY'S LONG TRUMP. IN EFFECT, YOU ARE MAKING THE DUMMY THE LONG HAND BY SHORTENING THE ORIGINAL LONG HAND TO FEWER TRUMPS THAN THE ORIGINAL SHORT HAND. EASIER DONE THAN EXPLAINED.

2. NOTICE HOW MUCH CARE YOU MUST TAKE TO RID YOURSELF OF A FOURTH ROUND LOSER. IT EITHER HAS TO GO ON A TRUMP (DUMMY REVERSAL), OR IT HAS TO BE RUFFED IN DUMMY, (DRAWING AS MANY TRUMPS AS POSSIBLE FIRST) OR IT HAS TO GO ON A SIDE SUIT WINNER, OR THE SUIT HAS TO BREAK 3-3, OR YOU WILL FINALLY WIND UP LOSING THE ¢*&$%# TRICK.

(102) EASY DOES IT

East-West vulnerable
Dealer South

North
♠ K J
♡ K 10 9 8 7
♢ 7 6 4
♣ K J 10

South
♠ 8 7 4 2
♡ A 6 5 4
♢ K Q J
♣ A Q

South	West	North	East
1 NT	Pass	2 ♢*	Pass
2 ♡	Pass	3 NT	Pass
4 ♡	All Pass		

*Jacoby Transfer

Opening lead: ♢ 10

East wins the ace and returns a diamond. You play the ace of hearts and a second heart towards the king, West shedding a diamond on the second round of hearts.

What is your plan and how do you play the spades?

EASY DOES IT (Solution)

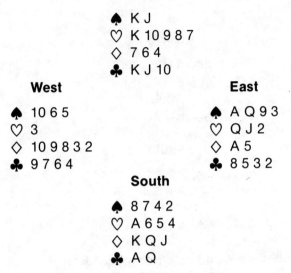

North
♠ K J
♡ K 10 9 8 7
♢ 7 6 4
♣ K J 10

West
♠ 10 6 5
♡ 3
♢ 10 9 8 3 2
♣ 9 7 6 4

East
♠ A Q 9 3
♡ Q J 2
♢ A 5
♣ 8 5 3 2

South
♠ 8 7 4 2
♡ A 6 5 4
♢ K Q J
♣ A Q

Your plan should be NOT to play spades! Force East either to lead a spade or give you a ruff and a sluff. Here's how it works: Once you know that trumps are breaking 3-1 and you have an inevitable loser in that suit, use that loser to your advantage.

After winning the king of hearts, strip the clubs, discarding a spade on the third club and play a high diamond. If East trumps he must either give you a ruff and a sluff or lead a spade up to the K J. He will probably discard if he happens to be out of diamonds. No matter.

Simply exit with a trump. East has no recourse upon winning the trick. He must play either a spade or a club. If he plays a club you must ruff in your hand and discard the jack of spades from dummy. In either case you lose only one spade trick and make your game.

KEY LESSON POINTERS

1. TRY TO USE INEVITABLE TRUMP LOSERS TO YOUR ADVANTAGE.
2. IF ONE OPPONENT HAS A HIGH TRUMP, TRY TO STRIP HIS HAND OF SAFE EXITS BEFORE EXITING WITH A TRUMP. IF YOU CAN, YOU MAY GAIN A TRICK FROM THE RETURN.
3. AVOID LEADING SUITS WHERE YOU HAVE TO GUESS WHAT TO DO, FORCE THEM TO LEAD THE SUIT, IF POSSIBLE.

(103) HURRY!

Both sides vulnerable
Dealer South

North
- ♠ 7 6 5 3
- ♡ K Q 8
- ◇ A 4 2
- ♣ 7 5 3

South
- ♠ Q J 10 9 8
- ♡ 7 2
- ◇ K Q J
- ♣ A K 9

South	West	North	East
1 ♠	Pass	2 ♠	Pass
3 ♠	Pass	4 ♠	All Pass

Opening lead: ♣ 2   East plays the Jack.

Plan the play.

HURRY! (Solution)

North

♠ 7 6 5 3
♡ K Q 8
♢ A 4 2
♣ 7 5 3

West	East
♠ 4 2	♠ A K
♡ A 10 9 4	♡ J 6 5 3
♢ 9 6 5	♢ 10 8 7 3
♣ Q 10 8 2	♣ J 6 4

South

♠ Q J 10 9 8
♡ 7 2
♢ K Q J
♣ A K 9

You have two spade losers, one quick heart loser, and one slow club loser. It is the slow losers that one has to worry about.

Notice that the diamonds and clubs are evenly divided between your hand and dummy—the worst possible arrangement—.

In order to get rid of slow losers in evenly divided suits attack unevenly divided suits. Hearts is the unevenly divided suit.

If West has the ace of hearts you can establish a heart winner for a club discard—but you must act before your second club stopper is removed.

Win the Ace of clubs and lead a low heart. If West wins you have established a heart winner for a club discard. West does best to duck. No matter.

Reenter your hand with a diamond and lead a second heart. West does best to win and continue with a high club. You win, cross to dummy with a diamond and discard your losing club on the good heart.

Now, it is time to begin with the trump suit. If you start trumps earlier, East wins and returns a club. Now your extra heart winner does you no good. West wins the ace of hearts and cashes a club—the setting trick.

KEY LESSON POINTERS

1. WHEN COUNTING LOSERS NOTICE THE DIFFERENCE BETWEEN QUICK LOSERS (THE ACE OF HEARTS) AND SLOW LOSERS, (THE NINE OF CLUBS).
2. MANY HANDS DEVELOP INTO A RACE SEEING WHETHER THE DECLARER CAN GET RID OF A SLOW LOSER BEFORE THE DEFENDERS CAN TURN IT INTO A QUICK LOSER AND GRAB IT.

(104) GETTING FULL VALUE

Both sides vulnerable
Dealer North

North
♠ J 10 7
♡ K 7 3
◇ K 10 4 3
♣ A 7 5

South
♠ Q
♡ A 5 4
◇ A Q J 9 8 7
♣ K J 2

North	East	South	West
Pass	Pass	1 ◇	1 ♠
3 ◇	Pass	5 ◇	All Pass

Opening lead: ♠ K

East plays the deuce and West shifts to the jack of hearts. Plan the play.

GETTING FULL VALUE (Solution)

North

♠ J 10 7
♡ K 7 3
♢ K 10 4 3
♣ A 7 5

West

♠ A K 9 6 4 3
♡ J 10 8
♢ 5
♣ Q 10 6

East

♠ 8 5 2
♡ Q 9 6 2
♢ 6 2
♣ 9 8 4 3

South

♠ Q
♡ A 5 4
♢ A Q J 9 8 7
♣ K J 2

You have lost a spade trick and you have a heart loser and a possible club loser on the minus side of the ledger.

On the plus side you have two equal spades in the dummy, the jack and the ten with only one higher spade outstanding, the ace.

If, after you draw trumps (ending in dummy) you lead the jack of spades and DISCARD either a heart or a club you will then have established the ten of spades for a discard of your other loser.

Instead of losing a spade, a heart and possibly a club, you lose two spades . . . period.

KEY LESSON POINTERS

1. WHEN YOU HAVE TWO EQUAL CARDS ON ONE SIDE (THE OPPONENTS HAVING ONE HIGHER CARD), OPPO-SITE A VOID ON THE OTHER SIDE, YOU FREQUENTLY CAN SAVE A TRICK BY LEADING ONE OF THE EQUALS, DISCARDING A LOSER IF IT IS NOT COVERED. ASSUM-ING IT LOSES, YOU WILL BE ABLE TO DISPOSE OF YET ANOTHER LOSER ON THE ESTABLISHED CARD.

(105) CONFUSE 'EM

East-West vulnerable
Dealer North

North
♠ Q 7 2
♡ A Q 8 7 6
♢ 6 4 3
♣ Q 5

South
♠ K 9
♡ K J 10 9 5
♢ A K 8 2
♣ J 9

North	East	South	West
Pass	Pass	1 ♡	Pass
3 ♡	Pass	4 ♡	All Pass

Opening lead: ♢ J   East plays the seven.

Plan the play.

CONFUSE 'EM (Solution)

North

♠ Q 7 2
♡ A Q 8 7 6
◊ 6 4 3
♣ Q 5

West

♠ A 10 8 5
♡ 3 2
◊ J 10 9
♣ K 10 6 4

East

♠ J 6 4 3
♡ 4
◊ Q 7 5
♣ A 8 7 3 2

South

♠ K 9
♡ K J 10 9 5
◊ A K 8 2
♣ J 9

You have to lose two clubs, a spade, and a diamond. Your only hope is trickery. If the diamonds divide 3-3 you can establish your fourth diamond for a club discard. However, if they detect your scheme, they will cash their two good clubs.

Your best bet is to DUCK the opening lead, playing the eight, hoping for a continuation. After all, East did signal.

With a likely diamond continuation, you make the hand. You win, draw trumps and play off two more diamonds discarding a club from dummy on the fourth round.

KEY LESSON POINTERS

1. FREQUENTLY AT NOTRUMP, AND OCCASIONALLY AT SUIT CONTRACTS, THE OPPONENTS DO NOT LEAD THE RIGHT SUIT. HOWEVER, YOU CAN MAKE THEM THINK THEY HAVE LED THE RIGHT SUIT BY ALLOWING THEM TO HOLD THE TRICK. USUALLY THEY CONTINUE, LIKE PUPPETS.
2. BY WITHHOLDING SPOT CARDS THAT ARE SMALLER THAN THE ONE PLAYED TO YOUR RIGHT, YOU CAN MAKE IT APPEAR THAT YOUR RIGHT HAND OPPONENT IS SIGNALLING ENCOURAGEMENT, WHEN IN FACT, HE IS NOT.
3. WITHHOLDING SMALL SPOT CARDS IS A COMMON DECLARER STRATAGEM AND IS USED THROUGHOUT THE HAND TO CONFUSE THE DEFENDERS' SIGNALLING METHODS.

(106) TWO QUEENS MISSING

East-West vulnerable
Dealer South

North
♠ Q 3
♡ Q 10 7 2
♢ 2
♣ A K J 10 4 3

South
♠ A 2
♡ J 6 5
♢ A K J 10 9 8
♣ 6 2

South	West	North	East
1 ♢	Pass	2 ♣	Pass
2 ♢	Pass	2 ♡	Pass
2 NT	Pass	3 NT	All Pass

Opening lead: ♠ 5

You put up the queen—but would this hand be in here if the queen held? Of course not. East plays the king. Plan the play.

TWO QUEENS MISSING (Solution)

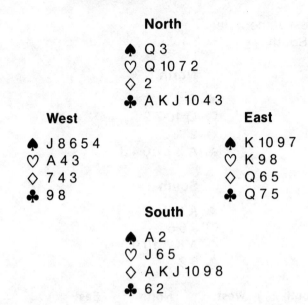

North
- ♠ Q 3
- ♡ Q 10 7 2
- ◇ 2
- ♣ A K J 10 4 3

West
- ♠ J 8 6 5 4
- ♡ A 4 3
- ◇ 7 4 3
- ♣ 9 8

East
- ♠ K 10 9 7
- ♡ K 9 8
- ◇ Q 6 5
- ♣ Q 7 5

South
- ♠ A 2
- ♡ J 6 5
- ◇ A K J 10 9 8
- ♣ 6 2

You have two powerful minor suits and if you can bring home either one for six tricks you make your contract. But which one?

Back to basics. When you are missing a queen in each of two suits, and bringing in EITHER suit will give you your contract, play the ace-king of the longer suit (clubs) and if the queen has not dropped take a finesse in the shorter suit, (diamonds).

KEY LESSON POINTERS

1. AVOID PUTTING ALL YOUR EGGS IN ONE BASKET WHEN YOU HAVE TWO POSSIBLE SOURCES OF TRICKS AND YOU CANNOT AFFORD TO GIVE UP THE LEAD.
2. IF YOUR TWO SOURCES OF TRICKS ARE SUITS THAT ARE EACH MISSING A QUEEN—AND BRINGING IN EITHER SUIT WILL LAND YOU YOUR CONTRACT—PLAY THE ACE-KING OF THE LONGER SUIT. IF THE QUEEN HAS NOT DROPPED, TAKE A FINESSE IN THE SHORTER SUIT.

(107) KEEP YOUR EYE ON THE BALL

East-West vulnerable
Dealer South

North

♠ A J 2
♡ Q 9 3
◇ 5 3
♣ A 8 7 6 5

South

♠ K Q 10 9 4
♡ K J 10 8
◇ 9
♣ K 4 2

South	West	North	East
1 ♠	Pass	2 ♣	2 ◇
2 ♡	4 ◇*	4 ♠	All Pass

*Preemptive

Opening lead: ◇ 2

East plays the king of diamonds and continues with the ace. What is your plan?

KEEP YOUR EYE ON THE BALL (Solution)

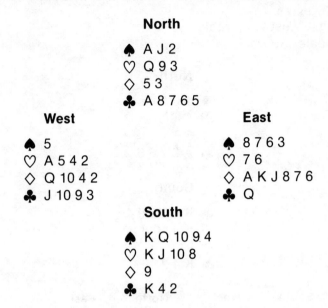

North

♠ A J 2
♡ Q 9 3
◇ 5 3
♣ A 8 7 6 5

West

♠ 5
♡ A 5 4 2
◇ Q 10 4 2
♣ J 10 9 3

East

♠ 8 7 6 3
♡ 7 6
◇ A K J 8 7 6
♣ Q

South

♠ K Q 10 9 4
♡ K J 10 8
◇ 9
♣ K 4 2

Counting tricks you have five spades, three hearts, and two clubs for a total of ten. Counting losers there is one heart, one diamond and one club for a total of three. So what's the problem?

The problem is that if you ruff this diamond you are down to four trumps in your hand. If trumps break 3-2 there is nothing to worry about. Just draw trumps and knock out the ace of hearts.

However, good players like yourself realize that sometimes trumps break 4-1. Very good players realize that when the opponents have been leaping around vulnerable, there is a bit of freaky distribution rampant.

What is to become of you if trumps break 4-1 and your ruff the second diamond? You certainly can't draw trumps and then play a heart. You will be playing notrump and all of their diamonds will be good!

No, you will have to work with your hearts after drawing but two rounds of trumps. Now they might be able to arrange a heart ruff by ducking once. You then lose a diamond, a heart, and heart ruff and a club.

The answer is to discard a club at trick two, a sure loser in any case. If they shift to a club, (as good as anything) you win, draw FOUR rounds of trumps and knock out the ace of hearts.

KEY LESSON POINTERS

1. WHEN FACED WITH A DEFENSE, THAT IS FORCING YOU TO TRUMP, CONSIDER DISCARDING A LOSER INSTEAD.
2. TRUMPS BREAK 3-2 FOR OTHERS, FOR YOU THEY DIVIDE 4-1.

(108) GOLDEN CLUBS

Both sides vulnerable
Dealer South

North
♠ A 5 3 2
♡ 9 8 7
♢ 9 4
♣ 10 9 8 3

South
♠ 4
♡ A Q 10
♢ A K 2
♣ A K Q J 4 2

South	West	North	East
2 ♣*	Pass	2 ♢**	Pass
3 ♣	Pass	4 ♣	Pass
4 ♢	Pass	4 ♠	Dbl.
6 ♣	All Pass		

*Strong and artificial
**Negative response

Opening lead: ♠ J

Trumps are 2-1. What is your game plan?

GOLDEN CLUBS (Solution)

North

♠ A 5 3 2
♡ 9 8 7
♢ 9 4
♣ 10 9 8 3

West

♠ J 10 9 6
♡ K J 6 2
♢ J 7 6
♣ 7 5

East

♠ K Q 8 7
♡ 5 4 3
♢ Q 10 8 5 3
♣ 6

South

♠ 4
♡ A Q 10
♢ A K 2
♣ A K Q J 4 2

You have two possible heart losers—if West holds both missing honors.

If this were a hand that could not be stripped before playing hearts, you should plan on taking two heart finesses. You have a 76% chance of making two heart tricks by taking two finesses. However, a 100% chance is better.

Your plan should be to try to coordinate drawing trumps with stripping diamonds and spades BEFORE leading a heart from dummy. Is it possible? Yes.

Win the opening lead and ruff a spade high; enter dummy with a trump and ruff a second spade high; back to dummy with a trump to ruff dummy's last spade; now ace-king and a diamond ruff puts you in dummy. Everyone is down to four cards. Both you and dummy have three hearts and a trump and the lead is in dummy where it must be.

Lead a heart from dummy and put in the ten. West wins but must either lead a heart into your A Q or give you a ruff and a sluff.

KEY LESSON POINTERS

1. WHEN THERE ARE LOSERS IN ONLY ONE SUIT—WITH MUCHO TRUMPS ON BOTH SIDES—STRIP THE HAND BEFORE PLAYING THE SUIT WITH THE LOSERS.
2. THE STRIPPING PROCESS ENTAILS A BIT OF PLANNING. SOMETIMES YOU MUST BEGIN STRIPPING BEFORE DRAWING TRUMPS TO CATER TO ENTRY PROBLEMS.
3. AFTER STRIPPING A HAND THAT HAS LOSERS IN ONLY ONE SUIT, YOU MUST PLAN TO WIND UP IN THE PROPER HAND SO THAT YOU CAN LEAD FROM WEAKNESS TOWARDS STRENGTH. OTHERWISE— MISERY.

(109) TRUST

Both sides vulnerable
Dealer South

North
♠ 10 5 3
♡ 8 3
◇ A 10 9 7 5
♣ J 8 5

South
♠ A 9
♡ A K Q
◇ Q J 2
♣ K Q 10 7 4

South	West	North	East
2 NT	Pass	3 NT	All Pass

Opening lead: ♠ 4

You play low from dummy and East produces the queen. Is there any reason to hold up? What is your plan?

TRUST (Solution)

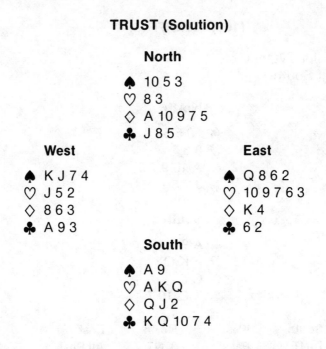

North

♠ 10 5 3
♡ 8 3
♢ A 10 9 7 5
♣ J 8 5

West

♠ K J 7 4
♡ J 5 2
♢ 8 6 3
♣ A 9 3

East

♠ Q 8 6 2
♡ 10 9 7 6 3
♢ K 4
♣ 6 2

South

♠ A 9
♡ A K Q
♢ Q J 2
♣ K Q 10 7 4

There is a very good reason to hold up. It is important for you to know how THEIR spades are breaking. If their spades are breaking 4-4, it will be safe to knock out the ace of clubs. You lose three spades plus one club.

However, if their spades are breaking 5-3, then it would be suicide to try to knock out the ace of clubs. Somebody would win and somebody or somebody's partner would cash a total of four spade tricks or five tricks in all.

The answer is to duck and watch carefully the card that East returns at trick two. If he returns the deuce, the only spade spot lower than the one led, you know that their spades are dividing 4-4 and clubs is the proper suit to attack.

If East returns a higher spade indicating a three card holding, attack diamonds rather than clubs. P.S. Don't worry about the opponents fooling you with dishonest returns.

KEY LESSON POINTERS

1. WHEN IT IS CRITICAL TO KNOW HOW THE SUIT THEY HAVE LED IS DIVIDING, WATCH THIRD HAND'S RETURN CAREFULLY. IF HE RETURNS THE LOWEST MISSING CARD IT INDICATES HE STARTED WITH EITHER TWO OR FOUR CARDS IN THE SUIT. IF HE RETURNS A HIGH SPOT CARD OR AN HONOR IT USUALLY MEANS HE STARTED WITH EITHER TWO OR THREE CARDS IN THE SUIT.
2. ALWAYS KEEP TRACK OF THE NUMBER OF TRICKS THE OPPONENTS CAN TAKE AT ANY GIVEN MOMENT. THAT CHANGING FIGURE FREQUENTLY DETERMINES YOUR CHOICE OF PLAYS.

(110) IT ONLY HURTS FOR A MOMENT

East-West vulnerable
Dealer South

North
♠ 10 9 4
♡ A K Q 7
♢ 8 7 6
♣ 9 5 4

South
♠ A K Q 8 7 6
♡ —
♢ A 5 3 2
♣ A 7 6

South	West	North	East
1 ♠	Pass	2 ♠	Pass
3 ♢	Pass	3 ♡	Pass
4 ♠	All Pass		

Opening lead: ♣ K East plays the deuce.

Plan the play.

IT ONLY HURTS FOR A MOMENT (Solution)

North
♠ 10 9 4
♡ A K Q 7
♢ 8 7 6
♣ 9 5 4

West
♠ J 3 2
♡ 10 6 4
♢ J 9 4
♣ K Q J 3

East
♠ 5
♡ J 9 8 5 3 2
♢ K Q 10
♣ 10 8 2

South
♠ A K Q 8 7 6
♡ —
♢ A 5 3 2
♣ A 7 6

Counting tricks, you have six spades, three hearts and two aces for eleven. Of course there is a slight hitch—you might have trouble getting to three of your heart tricks.

Counting losers you have three possible diamond losers along with two club losers, but you do have three extra winners in hearts.

The problem, of course, is how to use your heart tricks without running over to the other side of the table. If the jack of spades falls singleton or doubleton there is no problem. The ten of spades will be the entry. But what if it doesn't?

The safest way is to give up a spade in order to make sure you get over there. Win the ace of clubs, cash the ace of spades and if no jack falls, lead a LOW spade towards the ten-nine. Somebody will win the jack and cash two clubs but the show is over. You win the probable diamond shift, enter dummy with a trump and discard your three diamond losers on your three heart winners.

KEY LESSON POINTERS

1. YOU MUST LEARN TO BE GENEROUS IN THIS GAME. SOMETIMES, IN ORDER TO CREATE A SURE ENTRY TO DUMMY, YOU MUST CONCEDE A TRICK THAT OTHERWISE MIGHT NOT BE LOST. NO MATTER, IF YOU GET BACK MORE THAN YOU GIVE UP, DO IT.
2. THE TRUMP SUIT IS A FREQUENT SOURCE OF ENTRY CREATING PLAYS. NOTICE YOUR TRUMP SPOT CARDS. SOMETIMES THE LOW ONES ARE MORE VALUABLE THAN THE HIGH ONES!

(111) NO TIME TO RHYME

East-West vulnerable
Dealer North

North

♠ 3 2
♡ A 9 4 2
◇ A J 10 8 3
♣ A 10

South

♠ K J 9
◇ K 3
◇ K 9 5 2
♣ K 6 5 3

North	East	South	West
1 ◇	Pass	2 NT	Pass
3 NT	All Pass		

Opening lead: ♠ 7   East plays the ten.

Plan the play.

NO TIME TO RHYME (Solution)

North

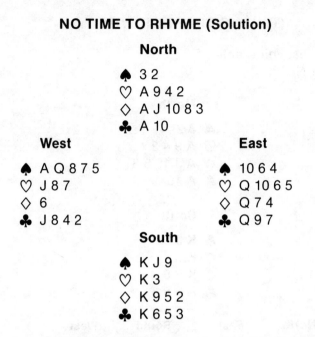

♠ 3 2
♡ A 9 4 2
◇ A J 10 8 3
♣ A 10

West

♠ A Q 8 7 5
♡ J 8 7
◇ 6
♣ J 8 4 2

East

♠ 10 6 4
♡ Q 10 6 5
◇ Q 7 4
♣ Q 9 7

South

♠ K J 9
♡ K 3
◇ K 9 5 2
♣ K 6 5 3

You have five sure tricks outside of your strongest suit, diamonds—one spade, two hearts and two clubs. Therefore you need only four tricks from the diamond suit to make your game.

You know from the lead and East's play to the first trick that West has the missing spade honors. (Third hand plays high and the rule of eleven tells you that East has only one spade higher than the seven).

Knowing that West has the A Q of spades makes EAST the DANGER hand. It is East, not West, who can hurt you if he gets the lead. Your plan should be to keep East off lead.

Lead a diamond to the ace and run the jack of diamonds at trick three. Even if it loses you have nine tricks and are safe from a spade attack with West on lead.

KEY LESSON POINTERS

1. PLACE THE MISSING HONORS IN THE SUIT LED BY BOTH USING THE RULE OF ELEVEN (ASSUMING YOUR OPPONENTS ARE LEADING FOURTH HIGHEST) AND NOTICING THE CARD PLAYED BY THIRD HAND TO THE FIRST TRICK.
2. WHEN YOU HAVE A VULNERABLE HONOR COMBINATION (USUALLY A KING) IT IS THE HAND THAT CAN LEAD THROUGH YOUR HONOR THAT IS THE DANGER HAND, NOT THE HAND THAT IS SITTING OVER YOUR KING WITH THE ACE.
3. PLAN YOUR PLAY SO AS TO KEEP THE DANGER HAND OFF LEAD— EVEN IF IT MEANS ABANDONING A CHERISHED RHYME—EIGHT EVER AND NINE NEVER. EIGHT EVER AND NINE NEVER REFERS TO A NINE CARD SUIT MISSING THE QUEEN WHEN THERE IS NO OTHER PROBLEM ON THE HAND. VERY FEW HANDS HAVE NO OTHER PROBLEM!

(112) WHOA!

Both sides vulnerable
Dealer South

North

♠ A 5 4 3
♡ A 8 6 3 2
♢ Q 4
♣ K J

South

♠ J 8 7 6
♡ 4
♢ A K J 10 9 8
♣ A 3

South	West	North	East
1 ♢	Pass	1 ♡	Pass
1 ♠	Pass	4 ♠	All Pass

Opening lead: ♡ Q

Would you rather be in 3 NT? Start thinking like that and you will wind up playing the hand as if you were in three notrump.

You are in four spades. Concentrate on the problem at hand. East plays the seven of hearts at trick one. Plan the play.

WHOA! (Solution)

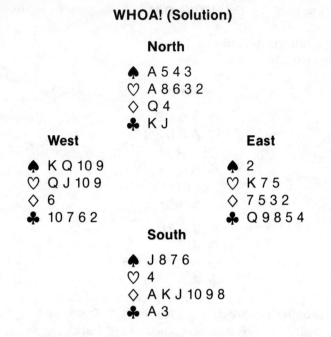

North
♠ A 5 4 3
♡ A 8 6 3 2
♢ Q 4
♣ K J

West
♠ K Q 10 9
♡ Q J 10 9
♢ 6
♣ 10 7 6 2

East
♠ 2
♡ K 7 5
♢ 7 5 3 2
♣ Q 9 8 5 4

South
♠ J 8 7 6
♡ 4
♢ A K J 10 9 8
♣ A 3

Win the ace of hearts, cash the ace of spades and begin playing diamonds. You lose three spade tricks and no more. It's that simple.

KEY LESSON POINTERS

1. WHEN PLAYING A HAND WITH A SOLID SIDE SUIT WITH NO LOSERS OUTSIDE THE TRUMP SUIT, ASK YOURSELF HOW MANY TRUMP TRICKS YOU CAN AFFORD TO LOSE.
2. FOR EXAMPLE, HERE YOU CAN AFFORD TO LOSE AS MANY AS THREE TRUMP TRICKS. WHAT YOU CAN'T AFFORD, IS TO LOSE CONTROL.
3. ON THIS HAND, THERE ARE TWO WAYS OF LOSING CONTROL. IF YOU PLAY ACE AND A SPADE, WEST CONTINUES PLAYING YOUR GAME, DRAWING YOUR TRUMPS AND THEN RUNNING THREE MORE HEART TRICKS. DOWN THREE.

   ALTERNATELY, IF YOU DUCK A SPADE, RUFF THE HEART RETURN AND THEN PLAY THE ACE OF SPADES YOU ARE NOT MUCH BETTER OFF. WHEN YOU BEGIN TO PLAY DIAMONDS, WEST WILL RUFF, DRAW YOUR LAST TRUMP AND THEN SCORE TWO HEART TRICKS. DOWN TWO. IMPROVEMENT.
4. A MAJOR TECHNIQUE IN RETAINING CONTROL OF THE TRUMP SUIT WHEN HOLDING A SOLID SIDE SUIT WITH AN OUTSIDE ENTRY, IS NOT TO LET THE OPPONENTS SCORE A TRUMP TRICK UNLESS THEY USE IT TO TRUMP A LONG SUIT WINNER.

(113) PUT ON YOUR THINKING CAP

East-West vulnerable
Dealer West

North
- ♠ 8 7 4 2
- ♡ A 6 5
- ◇ 8 3
- ♣ A J 7 4

South
- ♠ A Q 6
- ♡ K J 4
- ◇ 7
- ♣ K Q 10 9 8 2

West	North	East	South
Pass	Pass	Pass	1 ♣
1 ♡	Dbl.*	Pass	3 ♣
3 ◇	4 ♣	4 ◇	4 ♠
Pass	5 ♣	All Pass	

*Negative double promising four spades.

Opening lead: ◇ K

West continues with the ace of diamonds, East playing high-low. You ruff the second diamond and play the king-ace of clubs, West discarding a diamond on the second club. Plan the play.

PUT ON YOUR THINKING CAP (Solution)

North
♠ 8 7 4 2
♡ A 6 5
♢ 8 3
♣ A J 7 4

West
♠ 10 3
♡ Q 10 8 3 2
♢ A K J 9 6
♣ 5

East
♠ K J 9 5
♡ 9 7
♢ Q 10 5 4 2
♣ 6 3

South
♠ A Q 6
♡ K J 4
♢ 7
♣ K Q 10 9 8 2

You have lost a diamond and you have a likely heart loser as well as two possible spade losers. Is there any good news?

Yes. West has turned up with the two top diamonds and probably has the queen of hearts. West has passed originally so he cannot have the king of spades. This means that you have only one spade loser instead of two. None-theless there seems to be three losers.

Let's check out the distribution. West has overcalled vulnerable, twice, the second time at the three level. Certainly West must have at least 10 red cards along with one known club. West should not have more than two spades. Are you beginning to see the light?

Cash the king-ace of hearts, and assuming the queen has not dropped, finesse the queen of spades and cash the ace, stripping West of spades. Now exit with the jack of hearts.

West wins but remains only with red cards. Once he leads a red card you can ruff in dummy and discard your remaining spade. You are turning into some player.

KEY LESSON POINTERS

1. A PLAYER WHO PASSES ORIGINALLY AND THEN OVERCALLS AT THE ONE LEVEL AND LATER AT THE THREE LEVEL IN YET ANOTHER SUIT SHOULD BE AT LEAST 5-5 IN THE TWO SUITS.
2. WITH CERTAIN LOSERS IN TWO SUITS, IT MAY BE POSSIBLE TO AVOID THE INEVITABLE IF YOU CAN STRIP ONE PLAYER OF ONE OF THE SUITS AND THROW HIM IN WITH THE OTHER. OF COURSE THE PLAYER BEING THROWN IN MUST BE RELIEVED OF ALL SAFE EXIT CARDS.

(114) HEADY STUFF

East-West vulnerable
Dealer West

North
♠ K 8 3 2
♡ Q J 4 3
◇ 4 3 2
♣ 9 8

South
♠ A J 10 9
♡ 7 6 5
◇ Q J 5
♣ K Q J

West	North	East	South
Pass	Pass	Pass	1 ♠
Pass	2 ♠	All Pass	

Opening lead: ♡ K

East plays the deuce and West shifts to the ten of diamonds. East wins the king, and cashes the ace and plays a third diamond, West following with the seven and eight.

With five sure losers in hand, who do you figure for the queen of spades? Your contract depends upon a lucky guess—or is it a guess?

HEADY STUFF (Solution)

North

♠ K 8 3 2
♡ Q J 4 3
◇ 4 3 2
♣ 9 8

West

♠ 7 6 5
♡ A K 8
◇ 10 9 8 7
♣ A 7 6

East

♠ Q 4
♡ 10 9 2
◇ A K 6
♣ 10 5 4 3 2

South

♠ A J 10 9
♡ 7 6 5
◇ Q J 5
♣ K Q J

It is not a guess. West has turned up with the ace-king of hearts and East the ace-king of diamonds. Somebody must have the ace of clubs. Whoever has the ace of clubs started with 11 high card points and did not open the bidding. You did open fourth seat, remember?

If you discover who has the ace of clubs you will find out who has the queen of spades—the opposite hand.

KEY LESSON POINTERS

1. AS OBVIOUS AS IT MAY APPEAR, WHEN YOU OPEN FOURTH SEAT YOU KNOW THAT NEITHER OPPONENT COULD OPEN THE BIDDING. BESIDES, MANY PLAYERS OPEN THIRD SEAT A BIT LIGHT, SO YOU HAVE THAT ADDITIONAL INFORMATION WHEN YOU BECOME DECLARER.
2. WHEN THERE IS NO DANGER OF AN ADVERSE RUFF, WHICH YOU CAN SOMETIMES TELL FROM THE OPPONENTS SIGNALLING, (FOR EXAMPLE ON THIS HAND YOU KNOW THERE IS NO DANGER OF A HEART RUFF FROM EAST'S PLAY OF THE DEUCE) YOU CAN LOCATE CERTAIN HIGH CARDS OUTSIDE OF THE TRUMP SUIT TO HELP LOCATE OTHER HIGH CARDS THAT ARE MISSING IN THE TRUMP SUIT.

(115) THE SUBSTITUTE

Both sides vulnerable
Dealer North

North

♠ Q 3
♡ A J 5 4
♢ A Q 8 4
♣ A Q J

South

♠ A J 10 9 6 4 2
♡ K 3 2
♢ 3
♣ K 6

North	East	South	West
2 NT	Pass	7 ♠!	All Pass

Opening lead: ♢ 2

That's not you bidding seven spades, you know. That's a substitute. You were called away to the phone. You came back just in time to play the hand.

You win the ace of diamonds, and lead the queen of spades. When East plays low, so do you, closing your eyes for the moment. When you open them you see that West has discarded a club on the queen of spades. Plan the play from here.

THE SUBSTITUTE (Solution)

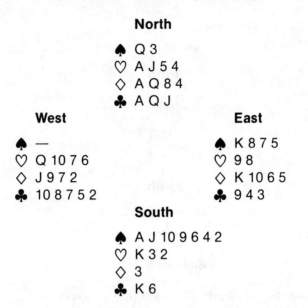

North

♠ Q 3
♡ A J 5 4
♢ A Q 8 4
♣ A Q J

West

♠ —
♡ Q 10 7 6
♢ J 9 7 2
♣ 10 8 7 5 2

East

♠ K 8 7 5
♡ 9 8
♢ K 10 6 5
♣ 9 4 3

South

♠ A J 10 9 6 4 2
♡ K 3 2
♢ 3
♣ K 6

To avoid the loss of a spade trick you must project the only possible ending, a two-card position with the lead in DUMMY. You remain with the AJ of spades, East with Kx.

You will then lead a side suit off dummy, East will ruff, and you will overruff to make your grand. How sweet. Not so fast. In order to achieve this ending you must reduce your trump holding to the exact same size as East's. Seeing that you have three more trumps than East, you must ruff three times in your hand and still end up in dummy. This means, in case you are not counting, FOUR dummy entries.

The play should continue as follows: lead a second spade to the nine, club to the jack; diamond ruff; ace of clubs; diamond ruff; low heart to the jack; diamond ruff; heart to the ace, high club, discarding your remaining heart, and voila—you are in dummy with only two cards remaining. A trump coup!

KEY LESSON POINTERS

1. IN ORDER TO AVOID THE LOSS OF A TRICK WHEN AN ADVERSE TRUMP HONOR IS PROPERLY LOCATED BUT NON-FINESSEABLE, REDUCE YOUR TRUMP LENGTH TO THE SAME SIZE AS THAT OF THE OPPONENT WITH THE TRUMP HONOR. THEN ARRANGE TO FINISH IN THE DUMMY WITH TWO CARDS LEFT IN EVERYONE'S HAND.
2. MAKE SURE YOU KNOW HOW MANY ENTRIES YOU NEED. DO NOT BE AFRAID TO TAKE WHAT MAY APPEAR TO BE AN UNNECESSARY FINESSE TO CREATE AN EXTRA ENTRY. IF IT ALL WORKS, YOU MAY SEE YOUR NAME IN A NEWSPAPER COLUMN!

APPENDIX   (Themes)

1. Counting Losers
2. Throw-In End Play—(Loser On Loser Variation)
3. Best Percentage Play—Combining Chances
4. Reading The Lead—Anticipating A Potentially Dangerous Shift
5. Placing The Cards From An Original Pass
6. Counting The Hand
7. Notrump Play—Counting Your Tricks—Entry Management
8. Notrump Play—Avoidance
9. Counting Tricks—Planning A Crossruff
10. Strip And End Play
11. Long Suit Establishment—Refusing A Dummy Force
12. Loser On Loser Play
13. No Trump Play—Counting Your Tricks—Ducking Play
14. Placing The Cards From An Original Pass—Early Discovery Play
15. One-Suited End Play
16. Deception—Playing Cards You Are Known To Hold
17. Notrump Play—The Hold Up With Two Stoppers
18. Long Suit Establishment—Knowing The Percentages
19. Loser On Loser Variation When Dummy Is Void In The Suit Being Led
20. Notrump Play—Avoidance
21. Card Combinations
22. Best Percentage Play
23. Counting Losers—Discarding A Loser From Dummy Upon A Winner From Declarer's Hand Before Drawing Trumps
24. Partial Strip And Throw-In—Counting The Hand From The Bidding
25. Long Suit Establishment—Entry Management
26. Planning A Trump Coup
27. Placing The Cards From An Original Pass— Concept Of "Needing"